IT HAPPENED IN THE
FLORIDA KEYS

Victoria Shearer

TWODOT®

GUILFORD, CONNECTICUT
HELENA, MONTANA
AN IMPRINT OF THE GLOBE PEQUOT PRESS

A · TWODOT® · BOOK

Copyright © 2008 Morris Book Publishing, LLC

Text design by Nancy Freeborn
Map by M. A. Dubé © 2008 Morris Book Publishing, LLC

Front cover photo: Wool sponges ready for the exchange: Key West, Florida, ca. 1930. Courtesy of State Archive of Florida.
Back cover photo: Florida East Coast Hotel Co., Long Key fishing camp, c. 1912, Library of Congress.

Library of Congress Cataloging-in-Publication Data is available on file.
ISBN: 978-0-7627-4091-8

Printed in the United States of America
First Edition/Sixth Printing

For Bob,
who has made my life's journey such an incredible ride.

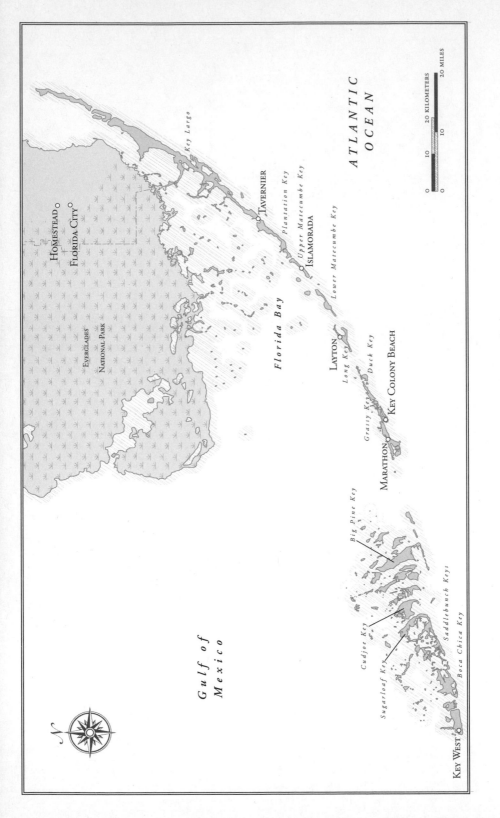

FLORIDA KEYS

CONTENTS

CONTENTS

ACKNOWLEDGMENTS

The Beatles got it right when they crooned: "I get by with a little help from my friends!" At no time has this sentiment rung more true than for the two long years of research and writing for *It Happened in the Florida Keys.*

My sincere gratitude goes to Megan Hiller for suggesting that I delve into the diverse history of the Florida Keys and write the book. And thank you to the gang at Globe Pequot Press, who continue to enthusiastically support my endeavors.

Thank you to the helpful librarians in the Monroe County libraries at which I camped out for weeks on end—Key Largo, Islamorada, Marathon, and Key West. The constant whine of my scanner could not have been easy to tolerate. A special thanks to Tom Hambright, historian in the Florida Room of Key West library, for his helpful insights. Thank you, as well, to Larry Kahn, editor of the *Florida Keys Keynoter,* for opening up the paper's archives for my exploration.

And finally, to my friends and family—you know who you are—thanks for the encouraging inquiries on my progress, believing my excuses when I said I was too busy to go for a walk or play tennis, and for those great pick-up meals when I was "down-under" writing. You are my inspiration!

INTRODUCTION

The storied history of the Florida Keys, like the fragile coral island chain itself, has always been indisputably connected to the sea. Revealed from its watery depths during the last glacial period, the Wisconsin, when the oceans receded more than 150 feet, the Keys remained virtually uninhabited until about 800 A.D., when Native Americans began visiting the islands.

And while the surrounding Atlantic Ocean and Gulf of Mexico have hosted a vast array of marine creatures for eons, the islands themselves—hot, barren, mosquito infested—have proved challenging and less than hospitable to the human beings who have chosen to settle here throughout the years.

From the beginning, the Florida Keys attracted a special breed of men and women—hardy pioneers who traveled the seas. Descended from early New England colonists and English sympathizers from the Bahamas, these Conchs, as the early settlers were called, led a hardscrabble existence for decades, as wreckers, sailors, and fishermen. Cuban immigrants joined the mix in the 1800s, bringing new skills of cigar making and sponging, and making an indelible contribution to the culture of the islands.

For seven generations, Conchs and Cubans have faced disasters—both natural and manmade. Philosophical people, they have weathered many a storm, stoically and with good humor. They are used to taking things in stride—hurricanes, fire, murder, wars, even a yellow-fever epidemic. The slightest victory is cause for celebration.

The Conchs and Cubans have welcomed strangers, as everyone who is not born in the islands is forever known. Writers, artists, dramatists, and musicians have thrived here. Presidents and foreign dignitaries have walked the streets. Armies and navies have called the islands home base.

Once an old Conch was asked why the people of the Florida Keys don't evacuate when a hurricane strikes. Matter-of-factly he said, "Son, we just batten down the hatches and let her blow. Reckon we're as safe here as any place whar [sic] there's blizzards, floods, dust storms, forest fires, and all sorts of things. We are as safe here as anywhere."

Safe the Florida Keys may be, for now, but strung from the mainland like a wisp of pearlized cotton candy, the islands are bound to face future threats, natural and otherwise, and unique events that make for interesting stories. Those stories have just begun . . .

HARD AGROUND

- 1822 -

NOVEMBER 19, 1822. FRESH BREEZES FROM THE EAST and a two-knot current set strong to the southwest spirited the eighty-six-foot schooner through the murky haze of the starless night. Lieutenant John M. Dale took a sounding about 9:00 p.m., as the 175-ton vessel headed north-by-east in the Atlantic waters along the Florida Keys. Finding no bottom at forty-five fathoms, he adjusted course to north-by-west and reflected on the events that had catapulted him to the command of this ship, the USS *Alligator,* a mere ten days before.

In 1820 the U.S. Navy had built a fleet of four twelve-gun schooners—*Dolphin, Shark, Alligator,* and *Porpoise*—designed to be small and fast enough to intercept the slavers and pirates that plagued African and West Indian waters. When the United States acquired Florida from Spain in 1821, the federal government resolved to use these schooners to patrol the waters off the U.S. territory's southern coast as well, in an effort to rid the area of marauders who posed a near-constant threat to commercial American shipping.

The *Alligator* captured several slave ships off the west coast of Africa in her first two assignments, then sailed to the Caribbean to hunt for pirates early in 1822 under the command of William H. Allen. Lieutenant Dale was second in command. The *Alligator* captured her first target, the *Cienega,* off Nuevitas, Cuba, in April, but didn't encounter any more buccaneers for months.

On November 8, as the *Alligator* was putting down anchor in the Cuban port of Matanzas, two men requested permission to board the vessel and state their situation. Captain Mayo of the brigantine *Iris* and first mate Marsden of the schooner *Mary & Eliza* recounted to Captain Allen how pirates had captured their two ships four days before in the Bay of Lajuapo, about forty-five miles away. The marauders threatened to burn the two ships and murder all the crew unless Mayo and Marsden secured a $6,000 ransom in Matanzas.

Having had no luck raising the money, the two men became intent on mustering an expeditionary force to rout the pirates and regain control of their ships. They asked Allen for his help. Having experienced no action for more than six months, Captain Allen enthusiastically agreed to lead the counterattack immediately. The *Alligator* and her crew of fifty left posthaste.

Approaching the Bay of Lajuapo the morning of November 9, the *Alligator* sighted three captured vessels—the ship *William and Henry,* the brig *Sarah Morill,* and the schooner *Nancy and Mary*—all at anchor. Under the sweep of its oars, the eighty-ton pirate schooner *Revenge* guarded the bay. Small boats full of men ferried back and forth between the pirate craft and the commandeered ships.

Captain Allen judged that the *Alligator* couldn't overtake the *Revenge* and ordered his boats hoisted out—manned and armed with muskets, swords, and pistols. The boats gave chase. The pirates fired a heavy round of grapeshot from their long twelve-pounders but caused no damage. Once in range, Allen's men opened a barrage of musket fire. The pirates abandoned the *Revenge,* jumping overboard or into their boats and making for a sister ship that had just entered the bay.

Captain Allen directed a midshipman and four seamen to board the *Revenge* and claim the captured vessel as its prize. Allen himself led the charge to the second pirate schooner aboard the *Alligator*'s launch. Lieutenant Dale followed in the cutter. His crew of seamen, manning the oars of the flotilla, joined the attack. More than sixty pirates, reinforced with small arms, cutlasses, and boarding pikes, awaited them aboard the decks of the sister ship. Gunfire raged from all sides.

Suddenly a musket ball pierced Captain Allen's skull, followed shortly by another shot that lodged between his left shoulder and breastbone. Mortally wounded, Allen shouted orders and encourage-ment to his men to his last breath. Under a continued barrage of musket fire, the pirates escaped out of the bay. Fourteen marauders were dead and a countless number injured or captured.

Lieutenant Dale and his men returned to the *Alligator.* They dis-covered the abandoned *Iris* and *Mary & Eliza* several miles away, adrift in the bay with their cables cut. Mayo and Marsden took control of their respective ships. Assigning his crew to the pirate ship *Revenge* and the other recovered vessels, Dale and his armada set sail for Matanzas. They buried Captain Allen at sea with full military honors.

On November 18, Lieutenant Dale, now acting commandeer of the *Alligator,* left Matanzas at 5:00 a.m. as armed escort to a convoy of American ships heading for Norfolk, Virginia. By noon of the next day, the brig *Ann Maria* had fallen behind and no longer was visible. Dale feared that if he stayed with the convoy and left the brig to sail on her own, she might come under pirate attack, and, thus, at 9:00 that night, he decided to adjust his course to north-by-west in an attempt to find the wayward ship.

It was 10:00 p.m. now, November 19. The *Alligator* was traveling at five knots. Suddenly, without warning, the *Alligator* ran hard aground on Carysfort Reef, off the coast of Islamorada. Lieutenant Dale was jolted out of his reverie. He called all hands on deck, lowered the sails, and hoisted the boats overboard.

Dale took soundings all around the ship, and deemed the deepest water off the stern of the vessel. He instructed the crew to throw the kedge anchor into the depths. Pulling hard on the hawser line, they attempted to dislodge the *Alligator* from its impalement, but the rope frayed from the anchor and broke, rendering the effort fruitless.

As high tide crested at daybreak, Dale and the crew made another attempt to free the *Alligator* from the reef's clutches. To lighten the ship, they threw water casks, guns, shot, chain cable, and ballast overboard, setting aside two carronades (short-barreled guns that fired large shot at short range). They managed to heave the bow anchor off the stern into two fathoms of water but succeeded only in pulling the bower back in without budging the ship. The crew then hoisted the sails in hopes they could force the ship off the reef, but to no avail. As a last resort, they disposed of *Alligator*'s booms, sails, and rigging, but still the ship didn't move.

Strong winds and seas battered the schooner all that night. About 8:00 a.m. on November 21, Lieutenant Dale spotted a sail on the horizon. He fired several signal shots and sent one of his boats to approach her. The ship turned out to be the wayward brig *Ann Maria,* which immediately came to their aid. Dale had exhausted every option to get the *Alligator* off the reef and finally, reluctantly, judged the ship beyond saving. He ordered his crew to offload everything of value to the hold of the *Ann Maria* and then abandon ship.

On the morning of November 23, after three days and three nights stuck on the reef, Lieutenant John M. Dale, with sadness and chagrin, set the *Alligator* on fire, both forward and aft, so that the ship would not fall into pirate hands. Safely aboard the deck of the *Ann Maria* alongside his officers and crew, Lieutenant Dale watched his ship burn. He had been her captain for only fourteen days. At 4:00 p.m. the *Alligator* blew up and sank to her coral graveyard. The *Ann Maria* sailed to Norfolk without incident, where Lieutenant Dale, the officers, and the crew of the sunken ship testified at a court of inquiry regarding the loss of the USS *Alligator.*

As per custom of the time, officials later named the reef after the USS *Alligator*—Alligator Reef. In 1857, the U.S. government determined to build a lighthouse on Alligator Reef but didn't fund the project until after the Civil War. Alligator Light was completed in 1873. Today, the hull of the USS *Alligator* lies in two sections on the reef, along with some rigging, cannonballs, parts of gun carriages, and a few bronze spikes.

DOUBLE CROSS

- 1827 -

DECEMBER 20, 1827. CHARLES GROVER STOOD IN dawn's first light on the deck of his schooner, *Thorn,* spyglass in hand, mesmerized by the ghostly apparitions hovering within his lens. Grover, the vessel's captain, was a wrecker by trade, a particular breed of Florida Keys entrepreneur dedicated to salvaging the bounty of ships that crashed on the reef, five to six miles offshore.

The coral reef—extending the length of the Florida Keys—lies hazardously close to the deep water of Hawk Channel and the Gulf Stream, the preferred route of ships traveling from Cuba, Mexico, and South America to Europe. The vessels, back then equipped with only rudimentary navigation techniques, frequently ran aground on the reef, which at that time was marked only by an occasional dimly illuminated lightship.

Wreckers were not thieves. They actually performed a public service, saving both crew and cargo of a sinking ship, often at great risk to themselves. By the end of 1825, wrecking had become big business in Keys waters ($295,353). It was a vocation regulated by few laws but governed by firm rules of honor: The first wrecking vessel to arrive at a distressed ship became the wrecking master of record, directing the salvage and earning a larger share of the proceeds. Other wreckers received shares in proportion to the amount of tonnage they salvaged.

The *Thorn* was anchored in the mouth of Caesar's Creek, just south of Elliot Key, along with the wrecking sloop *Surprize* and a fishing smack named *Florida*. Two other members of the wrecking consortium, the sloop *Capital* and schooner *General Geddes,* were about thirty miles to the south. Captain Grover judged his early morning vision to be about five miles away—a schooner with mainsail still raised and a larger ship, low in the water with no visible sails. Anticipating a wrecking bonanza, Grover ordered his crew of eight to pull anchor, hoist sails, and head to the reef. *Surprize* and *Florida* followed. Grover had no way of knowing, but trouble—not bounty—lay in the broken vessels he spotted aground on the reef.

At noon the day before, on December 19, 1827, the British warship HBM *Nimble* had spotted the Spanish brig *Guerrero* near Orange Cay in the Bahamas, apparently en route to Cuba. Great Britain maintained an antislavery squadron off the coast of Africa as well as in the waters of the Bahamas and the Florida Straits, which runs between Key West and Cuba. Great Britain, the United States, Spain, Venezuela, Colombia, and Chile all had banned the importation of African slaves by 1827, but thousands of ships still illicitly trafficked in the human cargo.

Cuba, a Spanish colony, still bought thousands of slaves every year to labor in their sugar cane and coffee plantations in spite of Spanish law to the contrary. (Each of Cuba's one thousand plantations had about seventy slaves.) Cuban government officials, with a wink and a nod, reaped financial benefits in each transaction. The eight-gun *Nimble,* captained by Lieutenant Edward Holland, correctly judged *Guerrero* to be a slaver and gave chase.

Packed under grated hatchways between decks of *Guerrero,* in a space only three- to four-feet high, 561 chained Africans huddled in intense subtropical heat in their own urine and feces, half-starved from the minimum allowance of food they were given once a day. (Another 150 had died during the voyage from Africa, from small pox, scurvy, diarrhea, or dehydration.) Ninety Spaniards manned the fourteen-cannon ship.

Nimble, with a crew of fifty-six, fired a two-gun warning. *Guerrero* could outgun the British warship, but the slaver's captain, José Gómez, noted strong breezes of a passing cold front and decided to try and outrun the Brits instead. About 6:15 p.m., ten miles northeast of the weakly lit lightship *Caesar,* which was six miles off uninhabited Key Largo, the two ships exchanged cannon fire. Thirty minutes into the battle, the copper-bottomed slave ship showed a light, struck her flag, and fired a blank, all signs that Gómez was surrendering *Guerrero* to the British.

Captain Holland ordered *Nimble* to cease fire. Gómez, however, had no intention of surrendering; instead, he suckered the Brits with a bait-and-switch. He sailed *Guerrero* away, faster than ever. *Nimble* took a sounding, which revealed only four to six fathoms (twenty-four to thirty-six feet) of water, but gave pursuit anyway. *Guerrero,* traveling at 10 miles per hour, soon opened a two-mile lead. Suddenly, at 7:30 p.m., the slaver slammed into the reef, breaking her masts and splitting her hull wide open. A cacophony of anguished, terrified screams echoed all the way to the following British warship. *Nimble* futilely tried to come about to avoid a similar fate, but five minutes later, brisk winds and heavy swells deposited her on the coral as well.

Guerrero turned on her side and began to sink. The Africans remained trapped in the hull; the ship's crew clung to the rigging. (By morning forty-one Africans had been crushed or drowned.) Holland and crew frantically threw *Nimble*'s anchors, ballast, and shot overboard in an effort to drift off the reef, but the outgoing tide firmly lodged the ship in place.

When the wreckers arrived on the scene that morning, Captain Grover spotted the two broken ships about two and a half miles apart. He ordered six of his crew to the slaver and another two to the ailing British ship. Samuel Sanderson, captain of the *Surprize*, attached a cable to *Nimble*'s bow, hoisted *Surprize*'s sails, and pulled the warship off the reef into eighteen feet of water. But *Nimble*'s rudder was completely broken and she was unable to sail on her own.

The wreckers began offloading *Guerrero*'s crew and its human cargo, transferring women first: 256 Africans and fifty-four Spaniards, including Captain Gómez, boarded the *Thorn; Florida* took 142 Africans and twenty Spaniards; *Surprize* accepted 122 Africans and twelve Spaniards. *Florida* immediately set sail for Key West; the others spent the night at anchorage.

Captain Holland worried that the Spaniards might try to overpower the American wreckers, so he destroyed all loaded ammunition aboard the *Guerrero*. The *Surprize* anchored nearby, flanked by the recently arrived wreckers, *General Geddes* and *Capital*. The two new ships fitted *Guerrero*'s rudder onto the damaged British ship, then finished salvaging the slaver. *Thorn* anchored next to *Nimble* to help guard the British ship's armament.

At 6:00 p.m., the wind shifted. Fearing *Thorn*'s anchor cables might become entangled with *Nimble*'s, Grover moved his ship slightly away from the British vessel. He then went below for his evening meal, a decision he would forever regret. Gómez and his slaver crew moved quickly, cutting *Thorn*'s anchor line and hoisting the mainsail. Hijacking the schooner and overpowering its crew, the Spaniards sailed the *Thorn* for Santa Cruz, Cuba. Unbeknownst to

Nimble or the other wreckers, the smack *Florida* had also been hijacked once it set sail, and it, too, was heading to Cuba.

To avoid mutiny aboard its vessel, *Surprize,* still at anchor, put all but two of her Spaniards aboard *Nimble* and successfully set sail at sunrise, arriving in Key West on December 22 with her two Spanish prisoners and 121 Africans (one died in transit). *Nimble, General Geddes,* and *Capital* arrived in the southernmost city the evening of Christmas Eve. Once Captain Gómez offloaded his African cargo in Santa Cruz (each slave netted him $300 at auction), he released the hijacked *Florida* and *Thorn.* The ships returned to Key West on Christmas Day.

William Pinckney, the collector of customs in Key West, seized custody of the 121 Africans that *Surprize* had deposited, pending a decision by U.S. President John Quincy Adams as to their future. In doing so, he ignited an international incident: The British thought they were entitled to all salvage from the ship *Guerrero,* including her human cargo. Disregarding Key West salvage laws passed in 1823, they refused to pay any salvage fees to the wreckers, not even for the assistance they received in being pulled off the reef. The U.S. held firm. The *Nimble* set sail, empty-handed, on December 27, but Captain Holland left Key West without paying the wreckers a cent.

The Africans fared far worse than the wreckers. Six Africans died in the seventy-five days they spent in Key West, one was seized as a slave by the captain of a U.S. revenue cutter, and the remaining 114 were transferred to the custody of U.S. Marshal Waters Smith in St. Augustine, where they were hired out as field hands at a paltry $2 per month. The Africans, legally free but forced to live and work as slaves, remained in legal limbo for years, primarily because U.S. laws dealing with importation had no provision for Africans accidentally landing in a U.S. territory. Finally, on March 29, 1829, the U.S. Congress passed legislation and appropriated funding to repatriate the Africans to Cape Mesurado on the African coast of Liberia.

The Africans set sail to freedom on September 30, 1829, but due to a combination of red tape, fraud, and incompetence, what should have been a six-week journey turned into a six month ordeal. Only ninety-five of the 711 Africans who began their nightmare aboard the slave ship *Guerrero* awoke as free beings on March 4, 1830, in their new homeland.

MASSACRE ON INDIAN KEY

- 1840 -

AUGUST 7, 1840. JAMES GLASS AWOKE WITH A START. A quick look at his watch showed 2:00 a.m. Not sure why he couldn't sleep, Glass looked out the door of his house on Water Street on the south side of Indian Key, where, surprisingly, he spied a large congregation of canoes beached on the waterfront. The revelation rocked him to the core—Indians!

Glass dressed and crept next door to warn his friend A. F. (George) Beiglet. The two men, who worked together as ship carpenters, slipped into the darkness, intent on alerting Jacob Housman, owner of Indian Key and proprietor of most businesses on the island. Glass and Beiglet crossed the public square and climbed the first of two protective fences around Housman's residence unnoticed. There, lying against the second fence awaiting daylight, however, were the invaders—more than one hundred Seminoles, led by Chief Chekika of the Everglades.

An Indian spotted the men and fired his flintlock musket, but the weapon merely "flashed in the pan." The misfire allowed Beiglet time to fire off a warning shot with his double-barreled shotgun, which was loaded with mustard-seed shot. He and Glass hollered warnings to the fifty-plus inhabitants of the tiny twelve-acre island as they ran off in separate directions to secret themselves out of range of the Seminoles.

Housman and his wife Elizabeth Ann had built up a virtual empire on Indian Key, which they purchased in 1831. Pocketing a fortune through shipwreck salvage and dubious business ethics, Housman built warehouses, wharves, tradesmen's shops, a thriving hotel and general store, even a ninepin bowling alley. He fortified the island against Indian attacks and cajoled Congress into providing naval protection on nearby Tea Table Key. Housman even suggested that the federal government pay him $200 per head for each Seminole he captured or killed, a fact that may have been the catalyst for the Seminole attack.

So, it was little wonder that Chief Chekika, having been tipped off that the naval cutters *Flint* and *Atrego* had left the vicinity of Indian Key several days before, assaulted Housman's residence before all others. By the time the Housmans reacted to the commotion at their doorstep, the Seminoles had swarmed the residence. The couple raced out the back door and scrambled over fences and rocks to the water, where they swam to one of their boats and successfully navigated in the darkness to the safety of Tea Table Key.

Meanwhile, the island awoke in terror. The Seminoles ransacked the Housman house with whooping abandon. Glass broke, muskets fired, and fire lit up the night sky. The Perrine family couldn't believe their ears. Dr. Henry Perrine had brought his family—wife Ann and children Hester, Sarah, and Henry Jr.—to Indian Key from the mainland, to safely await the final cessation of the Second Seminole War. Congress had granted Perrine twenty-four thousand acres on Biscayne Bay in 1838, so he could experiment with planting tropical and semitropical plants in South Florida. Instead, he bided his time working on the project on Indian Key, which he mistakenly judged was far from the hostilities.

Herding his family down the stairs in their nightclothes, Perrine lifted a trapdoor that led to a watery world beneath the house. The Perrines lived in the largest house on the island, a three-story structure topped with a cupola that sat on pilings above the sea. During high tide, water surrounded the structure on three sides. A short dock, used to off-load supplies, stretched from the house to the ocean. In the water under the dock, a labyrinth of turtle pens, called kraals, was connected to the cellar of the house by a narrow, walled passage. Seawater entered this passage during high tide, creating an innovative bathing facility the family could access through a trapdoor in the room above.

By this time, a large contingent of Seminoles had surrounded the residence, yelling and firing their weapons. Perrine commanded his family to crawl into the waist-deep water of the bathing chamber. He closed the trapdoor and pulled a heavy seed chest atop it so that the Indians wouldn't discover the passage. Ann and the children waded through the watery darkness of the passage near the turtle kraals and waited in fear and suspense. Perrine opened the front door and boldly confronted the Indians. Speaking in Spanish, a language they understood, Perrine announced he was a doctor, hoping that the Seminoles would respect him as a medicine man and, therefore, do him and his family no harm.

The family, huddled in the water below, heard the Indians shout and then leave. Perrine gathered his manuscripts and research notes and headed up to the cupola, where he thought he would be safe. The Seminoles, on the other hand, began ransacking nearby houses, pillaging all they could carry, and then torching the residences. Looting the general store, the Indians discovered a copious stash of spirits, which they consumed straight away.

Now drunk and crazed, the Seminoles returned to the Perrine residence. They broke windows, threw furniture, shattered pottery, and rummaged for valuables. Footsteps pounded on the stairs as the Indians headed for the cupola. Breaking down the door with their tomahawks, they discovered Perrine alone in the room. A single gunshot and demonic shrieks were heard all the way down in the turtle kraals. Henry Perrine was dead.

The Indians pillaged house after house, filling their canoes with plunder, then setting the town on fire. The Perrine house was aflame and the smoke began to permeate the watery sanctuary below. The tide had receded so much that the frightened group huddled in scant inches of salt water. The Indians, still whooping, hollering, and shooting firearms, ran back and forth on the dock above, loading their vessels with the island's stolen bounty. The burning house collapsed into the cellar. In danger of suffocation, the Perrines covered their faces with their wet garments, breathing through the dampness in an attempt to capture whatever oxygen was left in the chamber.

Tongues of flame flashed about the timbers of the dock. So as not to be burned by falling embers, the four coated their bodies with marl, a claylike substance covering the sea bottom. They were trapped. The pilings of the turtle kraals blocked their only exit to the sea. Manic with terror, Henry Jr., age thirteen, squeezed his body between two palmetto pilings and escaped, leaving his family and risking death at the hands of the Indians to avoid suffocation in the smoky dungeon. Hearing no screams or rifle fire, Mrs. Perrine plucked the courage to escape as well. With her hands she dug deep into the marl, dislodging one of the posts just far enough so that the three remaining captives could flee through the trapdoor of the burning dock and swim to shore.

When the Perrines emerged from the watery turtle pens, they found the island eerily quiet. The war cries and gunshots had ceased, and it appeared the Indians had left. Henry Jr. ran toward them. He had spied a group of Indians, still drinking in the general store, and discovered their partially loaded boat at the shore. With the bravery exhibited by his late father, Henry Jr. loaded his family into the vessel and, with only one oar and a pole, captained them to the safety of the schooner *Medium,* near Tea Table Key, where they were reunited with the Housmans, the Howes, and other survivors.

The Seminoles killed six settlers and an unknown number of slaves in the massacre at Indian Key and returned to their Everglades encampment with virtually all the riches of the island. Most of the island's residents escaped by boat or hid themselves in cisterns or high in trees until the invaders vacated the island. With the exception of the home of Charles Howe and a couple of slave hovels, the Indians burned the island to its foundations. Only a few families returned to Indian Key. Ann Perrine and her children moved to Palmyra, New York. Jacob Housman sold the island and moved to Key West, where he salvaged shipwrecks until his untimely death in 1841, when he was accidentally crushed between two ships. Federal troops tracked down Chief Chekika in the Everglades, where they shot and killed him, removed his scalp, and hung his body in a tree as a lesson to the rest of the Seminole tribe.

Indian Key has been uninhabited since the late nineteenth century.

THE KEY WEST HOOKER CHRONICLES

- 1848 -

SPRING, 1848. SPONGEBOB SQUAREPANTS, THE twenty-first century cartoon icon, lives out his daily adventures in a closely knit underwater society surrounded by an array of zany marine cohorts. In all likelihood, given SpongeBob's vibrant exuberance and colorful personality, he lives in the sponge beds of the Florida Keys, recently revived after a long period of blight. SpongeBob bravely faces danger in every episode, but if he would study his family history more diligently, he would know that the biggest threat to his existence is the same one that dogged his ancestors—capture by Key West sponge harvesters known as hookers.

Sponges are actually unique, multicelled, low-order animals that fasten themselves to the ocean floor in colonies and remain there throughout their life cycles unless forcefully removed. Said to resemble a head of decayed cabbage, the asexual animal has a headless, tailless, irregularly shaped body that is made up of a soft yet solid mass of tissue, permeated by a canal-like system that draws in water, filters it, and then releases it. (It is this filtering system that makes the natural sponge so absorbent.)

While sailing the waters of the Florida Keys in the spring of 1848, Bahamian wrecker William Kemp happened upon a prolific sponge bed. He gathered up a skiff-load of sponges, headed for Key West, and attempted to sell them, to no avail. Kemp judged the sponges to be as good as those imported from the Mediterranean, so, dauntless, he decided to gamble his future on his instincts: He took a shipload of Key West sponges to New York City. His hunch paid off handsomely. Finding an instant market for the sponges, Kemp sold them all and returned to Key West with a pocketful of contracts from New York sponge dealers. Publicly announcing that he would pay 10 cents a pound for all sponges brought into port, William Kemp single-handedly gave birth to the Key West sponge industry.

Immediately recognizing this as a potentially lucrative new business, turtle fisherman Alejandre Piestro financed the first official Key West sponging operation. Piestro hired a captain and a crew of hookers and scullers, who worked for only a share of the profits, no guaranteed wages. The captain sailed Piestro's schooner, trailing a ribbon of skiffs, like a kite's tail, to the sponge grounds, where the crew stayed for nearly six weeks. Upon arrival, the men built several ten-foot-square kraals (underwater pens or corrals), in which they would store the harvested sponges.

The skiffs set off at dawn. Each was manned by a sculler and a hooker. From the stern, the sculler propelled the boat through the shallows with an oar. Kneeling at the bow, a large sponge strapped to his chest as a cushion, the hooker looked for sponges through a glass-bottomed wooden bucket, which he held on top of the water with one hand. His other hand grasped a twelve- to fifteen-foot pine pole, one and a half inches in diameter, at the end of which was fastened a three-pronged, four-inch iron hook.

When the hooker spotted a sponge, he ordered the sculler to stop the skiff. Using the pronged pole, he hooked the sponge and gently dislodged it from the ocean floor, taking care not to damage it. The sculler squeezed the water out of the sponge and tossed it into the skiff. (If the water was at all rippled, the men would dip sticks into a bottle of shark-liver oil and swirl them in the water for about two hundred feet behind the boat. Within minutes the surface would become smooth.)

At noon the skiffs returned to the mother ship to unload their sponge catch and to have lunch. Days were long, hot, and riddled with gnats and mosquitoes. This was laborious work. After their brief break, the men returned to the sponge beds and hooked sponges until dark, when they again returned to the ship to unload and to have supper. The crew ate on deck amongst the decomposing sponges, which continuously oozed foul-smelling offal called "gurry." The offensive odor, like rotten garlic, was so powerful that a sponge boat could be detected a mile away. "Sponging takes a strong stomach and a weak nose," spongers liked to say.

Once a week, on Friday night, Piestro's schooner went to shore, and the crew unloaded its catch into the kraal, where the sponges would soak and rot. (A watchman stayed back during the week to guard the kraal from thieves.) Then, using a two-foot-long, four-inch-wide, five-eighth-inch-thick pine paddle called a "bruiser," the men beat the previous week's sponges to remove the black decomposed flesh and any small crustaceans or fish living inside the sponge. The crew washed the sponges in seawater, and, using an eighteen-inch needle and a fifty-six-inch length of sisal binder twine, they strung the sponges together and hung them on the ship's rigging to dry.

The dried sponges—now the mere skeletons of the former animals and a fraction of their former weight—were compressed and stored in the ship's hold. Once all available space in Piestro's schooner was filled with sponges, the captain headed back to port. He sorted his sponges into groups based on size and grade. Sheepswool sponges were considered the best, followed by yellow, grass, and glove sponges. He tied the strings of sponges into bunches called "wreaths" and stacked them in huge mounds on the public bidding dock at the north end of Elizabeth Street.

The sponge auction was held every afternoon at 3:00 p.m. An hour or two before the auction, wholesale buyers went from lot to lot, inspecting the size and quality of the sponges and making notes. The buyers especially looked for medium-sized sheepswool sponges, which, able to hold twenty-five to thirty times their dry weight and withstand the high temperatures required for sterilization, were much in demand by hospitals and the U.S. military.

Silent and orderly, the auction proceeded without controversy or incident. Writing their bids on paper, the buyers submitted them to an auctioneer, who functioned mainly as a neutral party. The auctioneer announced the highest offer for each lot of sponges. The captain of each vessel could either accept the offer or, if it was too low, could opt to store his sponges until another day.

As owner of the sponging schooner, Alejandre Piestto furnished all the provisions for the sponging excursion and, thus, received half of the auction proceeds. He divided the remainder equally among the crew, awarding the captain and the cook an extra bonus.

The buyers took their sponges to warehouse lofts throughout Key West, where each variety was sorted into floor-to-ceiling bins of like grade—size, shape, and quality. Men called "clippers" sat in front of the bins and, with sheep shears, trimmed the sponges of any clinging bits of coral. The sponges then were dunked in a bleaching bath and hung on drying frames for several days. Once completely dry, the sponges were stacked in Bahamian palm-leaf baskets and compressed by powerful screws. Finally, the lattice-encased, flattened sponges were corded into bales and shipped to large American cities and overseas.

The fledging sponge business, sparked by William Kemp and Alejandre Piestro in the mid-1800s, ignited into an industry firestorm that made Key West the sponge capital of the world for nearly fifty years. Sponging became the most important fishery in the Keys. At the turn of the twentieth century, the sponge industry employed more than 1,400 fishermen in 350 boats, who harvested up to 165 tons of sponge a year, netting $750,000 annually. And still, supply simply could not keep up with demand.

Key West held a virtual monopoly on sponge fishing in the United States until 1905, when Greek hardhat divers began harvesting deepwater sponge beds in Tarpon Springs, along Florida's west coast. The Greeks attempted to work the Keys shallow sponge beds as well, cutting the sponges with knives and trampling young sponges with their heavy diving boots. Blaming the divers for depletion of local sponge beds, the Conchs—as the Key West spongers were called—engaged the Greeks in barroom brawls and fist fights and even burned their boats to the waterline on three occasions in 1916. Key West became so inhospitable that the Greeks couldn't buy provisions in town without being accosted, so they withdrew. The Conchs successfully pushed the Florida state legislature to ban hardhat diving for sponges in the Florida Keys in 1917.

Key West hookers continued their prosperous sponge harvesting until the spring of 1939, when Mother Nature herself attacked the sponge beds. Fishermen noticed the water was clearer. The sponges smelled different. Fish, crabs, and turtles turned up dead on shore. A blight caused by a microscopic fungus swept across the waters of the Florida Keys, killing 90 percent of the sponge beds in a matter of months. The Key West sponge industry was dead.

The disease didn't affect Tarpon Springs, and it quickly absorbed the sponge market until 1947, when another siege of blight devastated its beds, a blow from which the area never recovered. The Florida Keys sponge beds returned gradually and steadily, however, and today the industry is making a comeback, due in part to a die-off of the Mediterranean beds in 1986.

Key West hookers work the same way they always did. "It's a hard and lonely life," says William "Sonny" Larsen, who goes out alone for a month at a time, trailing a skiff behind his twenty-five-foot boat. Watch out SpongeBob!

MUDDIED WATERS

- 1865 -

July 24, 1865. Dr. Samuel A. Mudd stood on the deck of the USS *Florida* as the 1,261-ton, wooden, side-wheel steamship approached the Dry Tortugas. Seven long days and nights had passed since he and Edward Spangler, Michael O'Laughlin, and Samuel Arnold had been spirited away in the dead of the night, shackled in leg irons, and ordered into the lower hold of the vessel, destination unknown. Mudd shook his head, still in disbelief, as the massive gun platform of Fort Jefferson came into view. Here in this six-sided, three-level fortress under the scorching tropical sun, seventy miles from Key West, on a mosquito-infested island with no fresh water, Mudd and his companions were condemned to live out their days.

Samuel Mudd had been caught in the vortex of a tornado since Good Friday evening, April 14. He had spent that evening quietly in his Maryland home with his wife, Sarah, playing the violin and smoking his pipe. The Mudds checked on their four children about 10:15 p.m. and then went to bed. Concurrently, in Washington,

D.C., an actor named John Wilkes Booth assassinated President Abraham Lincoln in the presidential box at Ford's Theatre. Shouting, "*Sic semper tyrannis* ("Thus always to tyrants," the Virginia state motto)," Booth dramatically leapt to the stage, catching his spur on an American flag that was draped across the front of the box. The assassin broke his leg upon landing but nevertheless ran from the stage shouting, "The South is avenged," and escaped into the night.

At 4:00 a.m., insistent pounding on their front door awakened Dr. Mudd and his wife. The doctor admitted a young man and his injured companion, who had supposedly tumbled from his horse and broken his leg. Asked to set the broken limb, Mudd cut off the man's boot and, upon examining the leg, found a simple fracture about two inches above the ankle. He set the break and fashioned a splint from an old bandbox. At Mudd's invitation, the men supped and rested until 5:00 p.m. Then they saddled up and, following Mudd's recommended shortcut through Zekiah Swamp, bypassed Bryantown and the Thirteenth New York Cavalry and headed into the Maryland countryside.

The following day, at church, word of Lincoln's assassination swept from pew to pew. Samuel Mudd told his cousin George about his nocturnal visitors. Alarmed, George urged Samuel to inform the authorities, but Mudd was curiously reluctant, instead asking his cousin to do the task for him. On Monday, April 17, three days following Lincoln's assassination and two days after Mudd's suspicious visitors had left the area, George Mudd finally rode to Bryantown and told the Thirteenth Cavalry about Samuel Mudd's encounter.

Through the subsequent interrogations and investigations that ensued, authorities connected the dots between President Lincoln's assassination and Dr. Mudd's injured visitor. Inspection of the cutaway boot revealed the inscription: J. Wilkes. Mudd claimed he had never met John Wilkes Booth before administering to his broken leg, but the facts suggested otherwise: Mudd and Booth had met on at least two previous documented occasions. The government concluded that Mudd knowingly aided and abetted Booth's escape. Authorities arrested Samuel Mudd on April 24 and charged him with conspiracy to assassinate President Lincoln.

Authorities found John Wilkes Booth at the Garratt farm in southern Maryland on April 26, where they killed him and arrested his young companion, David Herold. In all, the U.S. government arrested eight persons on conspiracy charges. The military trial, which lasted from May 9 to June 30, found all defendants guilty as charged. Lewis Powell, David Herold, George Atzerodt, and Mary Surratt were hung on July 7. On July 15, only three months after Lincoln's assassination, Edward Spangler was sentenced to six years and O'Laughlin, Arnold, and Mudd to life imprisonment at the federal penitentiary in Albany, New York.

So it was little wonder that Mudd and his three cohorts expressed incredulity as Fort Jefferson appeared like a mirage in the tropical waters surrounding Garden Key. This definitely was not New York! Unbeknownst to them, on the day of their sentencing, President Andrew Johnson secretly ordered their imprisonment site changed to the remote Dry Tortugas. The government, concerned that the assassination was part of a larger Confederate plot, wanted the prisoners far away from sympathizers who might try to set them free.

Assigned to the prison hospital, Mudd didn't find his imprisonment difficult at first. He wrote to Sarah: "This place continues to be unusually healthy, and the only fear manifested is that disease may be propagated by the arrival of vessels and steamers from infected ports." He hated the food, however: "My principal diet is coffee, butter, and bread three times a day. We have had a mess or two of Irish potatoes and onions, but as a general thing vegetables don't last many days in this climate before decomposition takes place."

After two months of imprisonment, control of Fort Jefferson was transferred to the Eighty-Second United States Colored Infantry, much to Mudd's distress. Samuel Mudd owned slaves to work his Maryland tobacco farm and strongly opposed black suffrage. He wrote to his wife: ". . . it is bad enough to be a prisoner in the hands of white men, your equals under the Constitution, but to be lorded over by a set of ignorant, prejudiced and irresponsible beings of the unbleached humanity, was more than I could submit to. . . ." Fearing for his safety, Mudd determined to attempt escape before the "Negro" troops could mistreat him.

On September 25, Samuel Mudd stowed away aboard the transport ship *Thomas A. Scott,* which proved an ill-fated decision. Probably the most well known prisoner at Fort Jefferson, Mudd was apprehended within ten minutes of boarding the vessel. And though the officers had not mistreated him before, his attempted escape brought down unpleasant changes in his routine. Mudd and his three unfortunate conspiracy companions—who had nothing at all to do with his attempted escape but were assigned guilt by association—found themselves imprisoned in an empty ground-level gunroom.

The "dungeon," as it was called, lacked cross ventilation, had slimy wet brick walls and ceiling, and an unforgiving slate floor. Immediately outside the only open gun port, all the fort's toilets emptied into a seventy-foot-wide moat. The odors were noxious and the food rancid. The men existed on stale bread and bad coffee. Six days a week, shackled in leg irons, the four did hard labor. On Sundays, they were confined to the dungeon. Mudd wrote to his wife: "My legs and ankles are swollen and sore, pains in my shoulders and back are frequent. My hair began falling out some time ago . . . My eyesight is beginning to grow very bad." The four men lived out this nightmare until January 1866, when they were again allowed to live with the general prison population.

Fate intervened in 1867, reversing Dr. Mudd's fortunes. Yellow fever hit Fort Jefferson like a hurricane. A viral infection transmitted by mosquitoes, yellow fever symptoms move quickly from headache, muscle aches, fever, and vomiting, to seizures, coma, and death. (Yellow fever gets its name from the jaundice many sufferers exhibit.) Dr. Joseph Smith, the prison doctor, contracted the disease on September 5 and died three days later. Samuel Mudd volunteered to help Smith's temporary replacement, the elderly Dr. Daniel Whitehurst of Key West, care for the afflicted.

For months, Mudd worked tirelessly alongside Dr. Whitehurst and the new doctor, Dr. Thomas, when he arrived. Regular routines ceased, as the entire fortress became one big hospital. Mudd caught the disease on October 4, and his roommate Edward Spangler nursed him back to health. Shortly thereafter, yellow fever felled Dr. Thomas as well. Dr. Mudd, himself still not wholly recovered, continued caring for the sick round the clock. In all, 270 of the four hundred persons living or imprisoned at Fort Jefferson caught yellow fever. Thirty-eight died, including co-conspirator Michael O'Laughlin.

After the epidemic abated, the surviving troops petitioned the federal government to release Dr. Mudd for heroic humanitarian services rendered. President Andrew Johnson, under siege by his political enemies for being too sympathetic to the Confederacy and preoccupied with fighting off impeachment attempts, ignored the petition. Johnson escaped impeachment by one vote, however, and, before he left office, he issued more than thirteen thousand pardons. Among the lucky were Dr. Samuel Mudd, Edward Spangler, and Samuel Arnold.

President Johnson granted Dr. Samuel A. Mudd a full and unconditional pardon on February 8, 1869. The good doctor, who always maintained his innocence, had served just less than four years at Fort Jefferson. Mudd was released from custody on March 8, but as his bad luck would have it, he had to wait on the island three more days before a Navy schooner arrived to transport him to Key West. In Key West, Mudd boarded a steamship bound for Baltimore, appropriately named *Liberty*.

Pale, frail, infirm, but nevertheless free, Mudd arrived home on March 20, 1869. He found his tobacco farm in disrepair and only partially regained his medical practice and his reputation, but he went on to have five more children with wife Sarah. Dr. Samuel Mudd, the most infamous prisoner ever to inhabit Fort Jefferson, died from pneumonia thirteen years later at the age of forty-nine.

UP IN SMOKE

- 1886 -

APRIL 1, 1886. THE ODOR OF BURNING TOBACCO permeated Key West in the wee hours before dawn, the skittering flames a cruel April Fools' Day joke. The wind blew strong from the south, the air unseasonably dry. The fire, which started at the San Carlos Club, on Duval Street, flitted among the wooden structures like a bee in a rose garden. The city's only fire engine sat in New York City, awaiting much-needed repairs, leaving the fire department—whose capacity and equipment hadn't kept pace with Key West's burgeoning population—only a meager hand engine with which to fight the fire.

The blaze raged out of control for more than twelve hours, racing in a northeasterly direction, completely destroying everything in its path. It catapulted along the waterfront docks to the U.S. Naval Station, where the military depot, utilizing its emergency firefighting equipment, finally managed to thwart the conflagration.

By nightfall, much of Key West was a pile of burning embers. More than fifty buildings had been destroyed and a significant portion of Key West's major industry, the manufacture of clear Havana cigars, had been reduced to ashes. The fire consumed six wharves, the U.S. bonded warehouse that stored all the imported Havana tobacco, the World Cigar Box Factory, more than eleven cigar factories, and countless shops and residences. Damages approached $2 million.

The Key West cigar industry sprouted its meager beginnings in 1831, when William H. Wall, a shipwrecked Englishman, built the city's first "segar manufactory" on Front Street. He employed fifty workers to hand roll cigars of imported Havana tobacco. In 1859, however, the factory burned to the ground and was not rebuilt. Other small, immigrant-family-owned shops—called *"chinchal"* or "buckeyes"—sprang up in its wake, each employing eight to ten cigar rollers and a couple of tobacco strippers.

It took a German Jewish émigré from New York City, however, to pioneer large-scale cigar manufacturing in the southernmost city. Samuel Seidenberg came to Key West in 1867, where he constructed a three-story factory surrounded by a cluster of cottages in which he could house up to two hundred workers and their families. (This "colony" complex concept became widely copied by subsequent cigar manufacturers in Key West.) He bought a tobacco plantation in Cuba and imported his tobacco directly to Key West. Seidenberg and Company produced authentic clear Havana cigars, selling them for two-thirds the price of made-in-Cuba cigars and reaping healthy profits. (The U.S. government charged duty on imported cigars but not on imported tobacco leaves.)

The American smoking public bought Seidenberg's product with puffing abandon, ecstatic to find a domestically produced, quality clear Havana cigar at a reasonable price. Seidenberg's competitors took notice and soon set up Key West factories of their own.

Vicente Martínez Ybor fled his homeland in 1869, after narrowly escaping assassination for his involvement with the revolutionary separatist movement during the Cuban Civil War. Ybor, regarded as the founder of the cigar industry in Cuba, reestablished his company in Key West, where it thrived. Cuban émigrés such as Eduardo H. Gato, fleeing the Cuban Civil War (1868 to 1878), followed. Skilled Cuban cigar workers poured into Key West.

The clear Havana cigar industry in Key West exploded. By 1876, twenty-nine cigar manufacturing "colonies" peppered Key West, employing two thousand three hundred people and producing one hundred seventy one thousand cigars a day. Key West had revolutionized cigar making in the United States. The city's relatively uniform temperature and humidity, similar to that of Cuba, ninety miles to the south, offered perfect conditions for storing, curing, and working the fragile top-grade *Vuelta Abajo* tobacco that made Cuban cigars so outstanding. It was the only place outside Cuba where the leaves stayed soft and pliable and didn't dry out.

Conditions inside the cigar factories were oppressive, however. Windows functioned as a light source only and were never opened to allow in fresh breezes that might upset the delicate humidity balance of the tobacco leaves. Strict hierarchy and a firm caste system ruled cigar production. Tasks were strictly defined, and payment was based on piecework.

Tobacco arrived at the factory either shredded and packed in bales or tied in bundles of whole tobacco leaves. Workers wet the tobacco and placed it in wooden bins to cure. Strippers, usually women, removed the center vein or *despalilla,* dividing the leaf in half, a task that earned them 2 to 5 cents per pound or about 40 to 60 cents a day. The leaves were sandwiched between boards and then sent to the selector, who divided the pressed tobacco by color. The shade of the tobacco leaf indicated its taste and strength: Light green was mild; dark mahogany tasted stronger. (Expert rollers used the best leaves to make the most expensive cigars.)

Bundled in groups of twenty-five wrappers, the tobacco moved on to the cigar rollers, always men, who sat at two-tiered tables. Highest paid of the cigar workers, rollers received compensation based on the type, grade, and amount of cigars they produced. The least expensive cigars, made mainly from tobacco trimmings called *picadura,* brought them $15 per thousand. A roller could make two hundred to three hundred of these a day. The finest cigars, on the other hand, were each created from a single tobacco leaf by only the most expert rollers and fetched $75 per thousand. A talented roller could make fifty of these in a day.

The rolled cigars moved on to the pickers who, using a method called "Spanish picking," divided the cigars into thirty-two shades. The picker chose like-colored cigars for each of four layers that comprised a box of fifty, picking thirteen of the finest and lightest color cigars for the top layer. He placed the cigars in a cedar box (the wood's odor kept bugs out of the tobacco), molded the box in a press to square off the round cigars, and sent each box to the bander. The bander carefully removed the cigars from the box, fitted each with an ornate paper trademark band, and precisely replaced them in the covered box.

To break up the monotony of this exacting but tedious work and divert workers' attention from the discomforting heat and humidity, factory owners employed readers, to whom each worker paid 25 cents a week. The reader, sitting on a high stool in the middle of the factory, read newspapers and novels aloud to the workers with a strong, expressive voice, in both Spanish and English. Readers worked in half-hour shifts for three hours each day. Employers felt the readings kept workers happy, helped increase production, and reduced labor tensions.

By 1885, eighty-six cigar factories were operating in Key West, twenty of which employed more than a hundred workers each. (E. H.

Gato Cigar Factory had five hundred workers and even started a mule-drawn streetcar line to transport workers to its factory on time.) The San Carlos Club was the hub of Cuban cultural life in the city. Still emotionally and politically involved in their mother country, Cubans met there regularly, plotting and planning ways to free Cuba from the Spanish and improve conditions in the cigar factories. By 1886, cigar workers were contributing 10 percent of their annual income to Cuban revolutionary forces, sending $20,000 to $30,000 a month to Cuba for use in overthrowing the Spanish government.

Though the exact cause of the fire of 1886 was never officially determined, evidence suggested that a Spanish arsonist torched the San Carlos Club and that intent was more sinister than an April Fools' Day prank. Spanish authorities oft complained of revolutionary activities emanating out of Key West, and police arrested two would-be Spanish arsonists in separate incidents mere days before.

The fire destroyed the Ybor and Seidenberg factories, among others, and put thousands of people out of work. The Key West cigar industry was down but not out. In ensuing years, Seidenberg and most of the other manufacturers rebuilt their factories (Ybor moved his operation to Tampa). By 1890, Key West had grown to eighteen thousand people, with Cubans the cultural majority, and the city regained its title of clear Havana cigar-making capital of the United States, producing an all-time record one hundred million cigars.

Cigar making in Key West began a gradual decline in 1911 that could not be stopped. Numerous causes triggered its demise: Labor problems and devastating union strikes significantly increased. Hurricanes in 1909 and 1910 destroyed half of Key West. The Depression left most smokers too poor to buy cigars. The hurricane of 1935 destroyed the Overseas Railway. Shipping and labor costs increased. Cigarette smoking became more popular. Machine-made cigars entered the market. And finally, the invention of air conditioning and central heating hammered the final nail in the cigar box. Climate control of the fragile tobacco leaves enabled factories to relocate in other more inviting areas.

Ultimately, the free Havana cigar industry shifted to Tampa. After a century as home of the most prestigious cigars in America, the Key West cigar industry finally went up in smoke.

BRADLEY'S BIRD BATTLE

- 1905 -

July 8, 1905. Guy Bradley snapped to attention as the sound of gunfire reverberated in the distance, breaking the early morning calm that enveloped his waterfront home in Flamingo, at the edge of the Everglades. The thirty-five-year-old Audubon-employed game warden gazed across Florida Bay, looking for the source of the shots. He spotted a familiar schooner—*The Cleveland*—anchored offshore two small rookery islands known as the Oyster Keys. "Here we go again," he thought, "Smith and sons are poaching my birds!"

Grabbing his .32-caliber nickel-plated pistol, Bradley kissed his wife of six years, Sophronia, and his two young sons—Morrell, age five, and Ellis, age two—goodbye. He jumped into his skiff and began rowing the two miles to the islands. He saw no point in hoisting his sail; the summer air was still as death.

Blue-eyed and clean-cut, Guy M. Bradley had been deputized by the Monroe County Sheriff's Department as a game warden in 1902, a year after the Florida legislature passed a law outlawing the killing of plume birds—snowy egrets, white herons, roseate spoonbills, and ibis. The Audubon Society, dedicated to stopping the slaughter of birds for fashion, agreed to pay his monthly stipend, $35, when it became apparent the state lacked the funds to employ officers to uphold the new law.

Bradley had hunted plumes himself for a time when the practice was legal, but, dismayed at the decline in the wading bird population of the Everglades, he chose, instead, to protect all the birds in the region from systematic slaughter. His territory was enormous—stretching from the Ten Thousand Islands and the Big Cypress Swamp on Florida's west coast, through the Everglades, and along all the Florida Keys to Key West.

By the beginning of the 1900s, plume hunting was big business, stoked by a huge demand for the feathers by the Fifth Avenue millinery industry in New York City. Milliners used the exotic plumage—called aigrettes—to create elaborate, extravagant hats much desired by fashionable ladies around the globe. Plumed bonnets had been the trend for decades, but in the early years of the new century, styles went "over the top" and so did the sums of money these feathers could fetch ($38 per ounce in 1895). Twenty plumes or more sprouted from some hats. Others sported wings, tails, or entire birds atop their brims. The most outrageous even included reptiles and mice, moss, leaves, and insects.

Snowy egret plumes were the most coveted because they were thicker, fluffier, and softer than those of other egrets and herons. Nuptial plumage, grown only in breeding season, was considered the very best. During courtship rituals or when a male bird relieved the female for nest sitting, the snowy egret displayed these plumes, spread out like a fan, extending from the bird's shoulder to beyond its tail.

The dedication of the "little snowies" to their young made them easy targets for the teams of hunters, who invaded the rookeries in groups numbering fifty to sixty at a time. The birds remained atop their nests, even in the face of danger. The hunters would enter a rookery, fire simultaneously, and slaughter the birds en masse. Then they would skin the birds—dead or alive—and remove their plumes. Predators devoured most of the orphaned egret eggs, but if an egg managed to survive and hatch, the young bird—unprotected and parentless—starved to death in a matter of days.

By the time Guy Bradley took his oath to protect South Florida's wading bird population in 1902, an estimated five million North American birds were routinely killed for use in the fashion industry each year. Shipments from Florida numbered as many as 192,000 skinned birds per carton. At that rate, an entire South Everglades rookery could be wiped out in five seasons.

Guy Bradley had his work cut out for him. He worked alone, without reinforcements, patrolling the waters of his vast territory and posting warning signs. He resorted to artifice on occasion, changing channel markers to throw the plume hunters off course and posing as a plume hunter to gather information on New York dealers buying illegal plumes. He even used his own money to hire a network of spies.

Bradley held no illusions about his job. Vilified by scores of unsavory lawbreakers ever since he had accepted this position, he had been shot at more than once. Today would probably be no exception.

Bradley had known Captain Walter Smith for a long while. Willful and ornery, sixty-three-year-old Smith, a Civil War sharpshooter, flagrantly poached the rookeries in Bradley's jurisdiction. Bradley had arrested Smith's son Tom, age sixteen, on two previous occasions, causing Smith to publicly threaten: "You ever arrest one of my boys again, I'll kill you."

Undoubtedly, Smith saw Bradley rowing his skiff out to the Oyster Keys, so he had plenty of time to set sail and escape arrest if he had so desired. Instead, Smith watched as Bradley slowly moved toward *The Cleveland*. Smith fired his rifle in the air to warn his sons Tom and Danny, who were in the rookery shooting birds. The young men were brazenly loading the dead birds onboard as Bradley approached.

"I want your son Tom," Bradley declared, citing a charge of violating the law by shooting plume birds. "Show me a warrant," shouted Captain Smith, "or you'll have to come on board and take him." Smith aimed his Winchester at Bradley." "Put down the rifle," Bradley calmly stated, "and I'll be happy to come aboard."

Two shots rang out. Bradley fell to the bottom of his skiff, which began drifting away in the strong current. Walter Smith and his sons quickly set sail and headed south without a backward glance at Bradley. Guy Bradley lay bleeding, as tide and current commandeered his boat. One bullet, shot from above, had pierced his neck and traveled down his back. Guy Bradley bled to death.

When he hadn't returned by late afternoon, Bradley's wife became alarmed and alerted Guy's older brother, Louis. Louis and another man boarded Bradley's steam launch and set off to look for the missing warden. The two men searched all night. Finally, at dawn, they spotted vultures circling the mangroves near Sawfish Hole. There, tangled in the mangroves, they found Bradley's skiff. The dead man had drifted for ten miles.

Meanwhile, Walter Smith had sailed to Key West, where he turned himself in to authorities. Smith claimed he and his sons were simply turtling near the Oyster Keys when the warden accosted them. Smith maintained that Bradley fired first, the bullet missing him and lodging in the mast of his schooner. Smith said he shot and killed Guy Bradley in self-defense. Unable to pay a $5,000 bond, Smith spent five months in jail while a grand jury pondered his case.

The Audubon Society paid for the prosecution's investigation, which revealed that all six bullets remained in Bradley's pistol and that his weapon had no powder marks, which would indicate that it couldn't have been fired. The only eyewitnesses, however, were Smith's sons, who—to no one's surprise—backed up their father's story of self-defense. Whether politically swayed to accept Smith's story or just innately suspicious of all government law officers, the grand jury decided, on December 2, 1905, not to indict Walter Smith for the murder of warden Guy Bradley.

Two weeks later, an angry crowd in Flamingo, led by Bradley's widow's brothers, torched Walter Smith's house and burned it to the ground. They knew Guy Bradley. He was the best shot in the Everglades. The townsfolk were convinced: "If Guy had shot first, he wouldn't have missed." Captain Smith and his family never returned to Flamingo.

Guy Bradley was buried on a shell-covered ridge behind a coconut grove, ten miles from Flamingo. A stone tablet with a bronze plaque marked his grave. The inscription read: GUY M. BRADLEY, 1870–1905, FAITHFUL UNTO DEATH. William Dutcher, president of the Audubon Society eulogized: "A faithful and devoted warden, who was a young and sturdy man, cut off in a moment, for what? That a few more plume birds might be secured to adorn heartless women's bonnets. Heretofore the price has been the life of the birds, now is added human blood. Every great movement must have its martyrs, and Guy M. Bradley is the first martyr in the cause of bird protection." (Hurricane Donna washed away both Bradley's body and his gravestone in 1960. The bronze plaque was later found and is now displayed at Everglades National Park.)

Bradley's unseemly murder, the first environmental homicide in U.S. history, sparked outrage throughout the country and called attention to the fledgling conservation movement fomented by the

Audubon Society. In 1911, the Audubon Plumage Bill was passed, banning the sale of all native bird plumes. The movement ultimately led to the creation of Everglades National Park in 1947 and the Florida Keys National Marine Sanctuary in 1994, preserves still dedicated to protecting all Bradley's birds. Courageous, conscientious, and "tough as a red mangrove," Guy Bradley definitely would have been pleased.

FIRST TRAIN TO PARADISE

- 1912 -

JANUARY 22, 1912. THE WHISTLE SCREECHED and screamed as engine number 201 of the Extension Special crossed Garrison Bight draw-bridge, spewing dense black smoke and clouds of steam atop the hordes of humanity lining the rails on Trumbo Island. The monster machine ground to a halt. Old, frail, partially deaf, and nearly blind, eighty-two-year-old Henry Morrison Flagler asked the time. It was 10:43 a.m., and the first official train of the Florida East Coast Railway Extension—Flagler's baby—had arrived in Key West. "Now I can die fulfilled," he said.

Henry Flagler made his fortune alongside John D. Rockefeller, running the Standard Oil Company. But by 1883, when he was fifty-three, his interests moved southward. Captivated by the idea of developing the wasteland wilderness of Florida, Flagler purchased two hotels in St. Augustine and, two years later, bought a short-line rail-road between that city and Jacksonville. He kept moving south, buy-ing up other railroads and building rail links between the fledging

Florida towns. Everywhere he built his railroad, Flagler created the infrastructure necessary to grow and support a cosmopolitan city.

In a mere ten years, Flagler's East Coast Railway reached nearly to Key Biscayne, in south Florida, where its terminus spurred the development of a tiny village called Miami. From here, Flagler vowed to extend the railroad all the way to Key West, which, at more than seventeen thousand people, was the most populated city in the state. In 1902, Flagler assigned William J. Krome and a team of engineers the monumental task of figuring out the logistics of constructing a railway across 160 miles of ocean, connecting the string of remote islands known as the Florida Keys with the mainland.

Flagler's fortuitously timed inspiration to connect the mainland with the deepwater port of Key West was no accident. Through inside government connections, Flagler had learned in 1903 that the United States was negotiating an agreement to build the Panama Canal. He knew that Key West had the best deepwater harbor south of Norfolk, Virginia, so would very likely become an important port on the new international shipping route the canal would create. Flagler envisioned his railway as the umbilical cord that would transport offloaded goods from the southernmost port city to eastern U.S. markets.

In 1905, at age seventy-four, Henry Flagler officially announced to the world that he would build the Florida Keys East Coast Railway Extension to Key West, funded entirely from his own fortune. People snickered and ridiculed the old man, calling his venture Flagler's Folly. In 1906, construction started in eighty-two work camps that were spread from Key Largo to Key West. Six years later, Flagler had the last laugh.

Virtually every citizen of Key West and hundreds of onlookers from all over the world thronged the vast expanse surrounding the Trumbo Island railway terminus, whooping and hollering and waving Cuban and American flags as the first official train to Paradise snorted to a stop. Many had never seen a train before. The Light-Guard Band began to play "Dixie" and Phil Henson's Ragtime Family Band struck up "Yankee Doodle." Firecracker-type "bombs" exploded. The Fifth Atlantic Fleet, peppering Key West harbor, blew their whistles.

Henry Flagler alighted from his private rail car, Rambler, onto red-carpeted steps amidst thunderous applause, and the "Over the Sea Railroad Celebration" officially began. The Extension Special included five Pullman cars loaded with such dignitaries as Assistant Secretary of War Robert Shaw, who was President William Howard Taft's representative, as well as ambassadors from Italy, Mexico, Portugal, Costa Rica, Ecuador, Guatemala, San Salvador, and Uruguay. (Seven more trains arrived throughout the day bearing other diplomats, military personnel, and politicians.)

Children serenaded the old man and sprinkled petals in his path as he made his way to the speaker's dais. "Do I smell roses?" Henry Flagler asked. Addressing the adoring crowd massed before him, his eyes filled with tears, Flagler recapped the twenty-seven-year construction project that began with the excavation of the foundation of Hotel Ponce de Leon in St. Augustine, traversed the sea of wilderness between Palm Beach and Miami, and finally bridged the ocean to Key West. "We have been trying to anchor Key West to the mainland . . . and anchor it we have done," he quite justly boasted.

Considered the greatest engineering feat ever accomplished to that date, construction of the Florida East Coast Railway Extension had been an arduous, dangerous, frustrating, costly (more than $20 million) endeavor. Nearly unbearable mosquitoes, stifling heat, no fresh water, repeated hurricanes (1906, 1909, 1910), low wages ($1.50 per day for a ten-hour day), injuries, and fatalities (more than seven hundred) plagued the workers—six thousand men from all over the world. Lifting thousands of tons of steel and concrete (each bridge required reinforced concrete arches made from special German cement that would harden underwater) and digging twenty million cubic yards of marl, sand, and coral rock for embankments, the men worked liked machines to make Henry Flagler's dream a reality.

Accolades were the order of the day. Key West mayor F. N. Fogarty presented the visionary genius with a solid-gold replica of a Western Union Telegram on which every worker and employee of the Florida East Coast Railway had inscribed their congratulations. Dignitary after dignitary touted the great little man with the big ideas, lauding the railroad that tethered Key West to the world as the "Eighth Wonder of the World."

Food and drink spilled from tents erected on the Flagler-made 134-acre Trumbo Island—wooden barrels of key limeade, coconut ice cream, turtle stew and conch chowder, Cuban pork sandwiches, and lots of key lime pies. As the day wore on, the celebration moved into the streets, where by nightfall, a snaking conga line ended up dancing in Cuban nightclubs. The revelry, which continued for three days, included a Cuban circus and a Spanish opera performance.

After the welcoming speeches, however, Henry Flagler slipped away to a waiting ferry bound for Cuba. His health delicate, the aging empire builder was simply grateful to have lived long enough to experience his triumphal railway journey to the southernmost point in the United States. Five days later he sent a thank you note to his general manager, J. R. Parrott, that said in part: "The work I have been doing for many years has been largely prompted by a desire to help my fellowmen, and I hope you will let every employee of the Company know that I thank him for the gift, the spirit that prompted it, and for the sentiment therein expressed."

Henry Flagler rode his dream to reality with little time to spare. Less than one year later, he fell down the marble staircase of Whitehall, his Palm Beach home, breaking his right hip. His health deteriorated rapidly, and on May 20, 1913, the man who built the railway to the sea died at the age of eight-three.

His passing foreshadowed a death knell for his railroad as well. After World War I, Key West harbor lost strategic importance. The cigar and sponging industries moved to mainland Florida, and despite the rail link, the lack of fresh water kept the Keys from developing into a major tourist destination. The Florida East Coast Railway Extension never made a profit and, by 1932, declared bankruptcy. As fate would have it, Flagler's dream creation lived only twenty-two years longer than he did. On Labor Day, September 1, 1935, a 250-mile-per-hour hurricane delivered the railroad's death blow, washing out more than forty miles of track and rail bed. Bankrupt and severely damaged, the railroad sold its right-of-way to the state of Florida to be modified into a vehicular highway. (The Overseas Highway was completed in 1938.)

An enduring testimony to Henry Flagler's extraordinary vision, many of the arched bridges that supported the railroad trestles still stand today. Long Key Bridge, Old Seven Mile Bridge, and Bahia Honda Bridge are listed in the National Register of Historic Places.

MOSQUITOES 1, BATS 0

- 1929 -

MARCH 15, 1929. FRED JOHNSON POUNDED THE FINAL NAIL into the cypress-clad structure. He picked up a plaque inscribed with the words: "Dedicated to Good Health at Perky, Florida, by Mr. and Mrs. R. C. Perky" and attached it to the concrete foundation. Johnson had worn many hats in his lifetime—wrecker, sponger, resort manager, plumber. But he had no way of knowing that building this 35-foot bat tower for Righter Clyde Perky would be his most lasting achievement.

R. C. Perky was a man of big ideas. A wealthy Miami land developer and the Florida Keys largest landowner, Perky bought a sponge farm on remote Sugarloaf Key in bankruptcy proceedings in 1925. After a brief unsuccessful flirtation with artificial sponge cultivation, Perky instead decided to develop the acreage, which encompassed most of the island, and create a utopian village and an elite resort fishing camp that would attract wealthy settlers and vacationers from the North. At the time, Sugarloaf was only a whistle-stop on Flagler's

East Coast Railway Extension, but the first road-ferry from Key West to Miami was projected to reach Sugarloaf Key by 1927.

In 1928, Perky hired Fred Johnson to oversee his construction projects. Johnson supervised the building of a roadway from Perky's property to the now-completed main thoroughfare (presently Overseas Highway). This was followed by construction of a generating plant, two water towers, and a large home for the Perkys.

Remote and isolated though it was, Sugarloaf Key supported an annoying population that R. C. Perky hadn't anticipated—mosquitoes. "In the late afternoon, you would just have to rake the bugs off your arm," said Johnson. "They'd form a black print on your hand if you put it against a screen and suck all the blood right out of it [your hand] if you let them. Whenever you went outside, the first thing you did was build a fire of coconut husks to try to keep them away, then you'd cut a palmetto leaf so you had something to slap them off your back while you worked," he added.

Perky realized that to keep the life from being sucked out of his venture, he would have to rid Sugarloaf Key of its mosquito infestation. The book *Bats, Mosquitoes, and Dollars,* by Dr. Charles A. Campbell, a Texas physician, provided his inspiration. For decades, Dr. Campbell had designed and tested roosts that would attract bats, trying to prove his theory that because of their insatiable appetite for mosquitoes, a concentration of bats would significantly reduce the mosquito population in an area and, therefore, control the spread of yellow fever and malaria.

After much trial and error, Dr. Campbell concluded that bats preferred to roost high above the ground instead of in boxes, and he began designing a bat tower. In 1911, he built his first successful tower near San Antonio, a twenty-foot-high pyramid structure mounted on four ten-foot posts. A crate of bat bait (Campbell's secret formula) was placed in a special compartment in the tower.

Within three months, thousands of bats had settled on the cypress-lath roosting shelves that lined the interior of the tower. Bat excrement rained down the central chamber of the Texas tower, where it was collected for use as fertilizer. Campbell sold more than four thousand pounds of bat guano the first year alone, at $500 per box, generating a significant amount of income.

The doctor's success enticed R. C. Perky to purchase Campbell's complex blueprints for a bat tower of his own. (Sixteen bat towers, in total, were built from Campbell's plans in the United States and Italy.) The Florida Keys had far fewer bats that did San Antonio, but Perky convinced himself that there were enough of the winged mammals on the island to make his project work.

In five months, at a cost of $10,000, Fred Johnson and three other workers constructed a thirty-five-foot bat tower out of Dade pine, an immensely dense hardwood that was virtually termite-proof. They covered the exterior with cypress shingles. The tower had a louvered bat entrance facing the prevailing winds. A guano removal shoot was specially designed to release just enough excrement to fill fifty-pound bags. With the inscription plaque firmly affixed to the base of the tower, Perky took a picture of the finished structure and sent it to Dr. Campbell, along with a check for $175 worth of special bat bait.

The bat bait arrived in a small box, several weeks later, by train. "The instructions said to pour four ounces of distilled water into each hole and then get the hell out of there," laughed Mr. Johnson. "I didn't know what that meant. I was half expecting it to explode or something. Then I found out what happened. It stunk so damn bad it could have killed you."

The bat bait in place, his mosquito problems soon would be over, Perky thought. He waited for bats to take residence in his new tower. He and Johnson built thirteen cottages, bungalows, and stores, as well as a post office, and changed the island's name to Perky, Florida. But, no bats came to Perky. No settlers came to Perky. Few fishermen came to Perky. The wait continued.

But, as it so often happens in the Florida Keys, Mother Nature intervened. The "Big Storm of 1929" washed over Sugarloaf Key, flooding the bat tower. When a year had passed and still no bats roosted in the tower, Perky decided the storm had ruined the bait and tried to order another box. To his eternal consternation, Perky found that, in the interim, Dr. Campbell had died, taking the secret bat bait formula with him to his grave.

R. C. Perky declared bankruptcy several years later. He died eleven years to the day the tower was completed—March 15, 1940—a poor man. Perky, Florida reverted to Sugarloaf Key. And bats never moved into Perky's tower.

Some forty years later in 1981, however, workers contracted by the Key West Preservation Board to restore the old bat tower discovered that finally some winged creatures were buzzing about in Perky's tower. Thousands of bees had colonized the structure, their combs dripping with mangrove honey. "We smoked them out," boasted Dale Merchant, a Key West carpenter repairing the tower. "We burned some burlap in an old bucket and it ran them right away. We just had to be careful not to set the tower on fire."

Today, Perky's Bat Tower stands as it did long ago—stoic and uninhabited. Though it never attracted any bats, the tower has withstood scores of hurricanes. Of Dr. Campbell's three surviving bat towers, Perky's is the only one in the world still accessible to the public. Finally awarded a degree of respectability, Perky's Bat Tower is now listed on the National Registry of Historic Places.

BLIND PIGS AND BOOTLEG

- 1933 -

DECEMBER 15, 1933. "BIG" SKINNER, THE three-hundred-pound bartender of The Blind Pig, handed his boss, Joseph "Josie" Russell, and Josie's good friend Ernest Hemingway two frosty mojitos for the toast. The United States government had just made an official announcement: The Eighteenth Amendment, the Volstead Act, which had forbidden the sale and manufacture of liquor in America since 1920, had just been repealed. Prohibition was over! Glasses clinked throughout the Key West speakeasy. Patrons and bootleggers cheered. Josie's Green Street dive, a favorite local nightspot specializing in fast women, illicit gambling, and Hoover gold (bootleg rum), had just become legit.

Liquor washed over Key West during Prohibition like high tide under a full moon. Given its proximity to Cuba and the Bahamas, both of which were swimming in booze, the Florida Keys became a wide-open liquor distribution point. During Prohibition, locals considered smuggling liquor a public service, looking upon the restrictive law as some futile fantasy of the federal government. Buyers came from all over the country to purchase the liquid contraband, which unlike hooch in other parts of the country, was rarely watered down. With Bimini only a hundred miles from Key Largo and Cuba a mere ninety miles from Key West, nearly every fisherman with a motorboat and a modicum of chutzpah cashed in on the booty. Rumrunning became a cottage industry in the Keys.

Josie Russell was one of a multitude of dive keepers and rum-runners capitalizing on the dry spell that had enveloped the rest of the nation for those many years. He had met Ernest Hemingway several years before, when the writer asked him to cash a royalty check for $1,000 that he had received for his novel, *A Farewell to Arms.* (The bank refused to cash Hemingway's check because they felt his demeanor was too scruffy.) Hemingway frequented The Blind Pig—named for the slang term used during Prohibition to define a small hole-in-the-wall that served bootleg booze—to buy scotch and talk fishing. The two men became fast friends, hanging out together and fishing for marlin aboard Russell's thirty-four-foot vessel, *Anita,* or cruising to Cuba to bring back bootleg.

As the Prohibition-repeal party swung into high gear, Russell and Hemingway sat at the long wooden bar and reminisced with their cohorts about the daring, adventurous smuggling escapades that had pitted their contemporaries against the "feds" for the past thirteen years. The Alcohol Tax Unit of the Internal Revenue Department sent federal agents, referred to by locals as "prohi's" or "revenooers," to regularly raid the speakeasy dives, and the Coast Guard set up an active operation in Key West to counteract the rumrunners. But the frustrated feds fought a losing battle: Virtually everyone in Key West was against Prohibition. Even those tasked with enforcing the law openly aided and abetted the smugglers.

In April 1926, seven Miami customs agents raided ten speakeasies in Key West, seizing several thousand dollars worth of liquor and arresting some of the dive keepers. The agents appeared before the U.S. commissioner, seeking arrest warrants for those in custody. What the agents didn't know, however, was that other victims of the raid were simultaneously appealing to Rogelio Gomez, the Monroe County justice of the peace, seeking warrants to apprehend the seven government agents themselves, under charges of assault and battery, destroying private property, and larceny. Gomez sided with the locals and granted the warrants.

Several Monroe County sheriff deputies stationed themselves outside the federal building, planning to arrest the agents upon their departure. A crowd of voyeuristic spectators gathered round. The seven agents glanced out the window of the commissioner's office, saw the growing crowd, and, sensing their unpopularity, decided to exit through the rear of the building into the naval station to avoid being mobbed.

They hopped aboard a Navy vessel headed for Miami, thinking they were safe, but when they reached the city's port, Dade County sheriff Henry Chase handed each agent an arrest warrant. The fight was on. The mess was finally cleaned up when the two sides—locals and feds—reached a compromise and dropped both cases. Rogelio Gomez, however, earned the dubious distinction of being the only county magistrate in the United States to ever issue an arrest warrant against a Prohibition agent.

Local rumrunners knew every channel, creek, and mangrove inlet the length of the Keys and used stealth and subterfuge to evade customs agents and the Coast Guard. Working at night in small, fast boats, runners in the upper Keys shot out to an area of international waters about three miles offshore Key Largo, known as Rum Row, where large vessels filled with contraband liquor anchored and waited to deal.

The bootleggers loaded their booty into gunny sacks and headed back to Key Largo without running lights. If the evening went according to plan, they would ease their boats into remote, mangrove-lined inlets and hand off their haul to mainland contacts who would spirit the liquor up to Miami.

Paul "Deacon" Lowe made his first liquor run to Cuba at the beginning of Prohibition, when he was nineteen years old. The booze runs took him at least six days, but netted him about $400 a run, a fortune for a Key West teenager in the early 1920s. Three or four times a month, Lowe and two crew members ran to Cuba, loaded his boat, *Runaway,* with hundreds of cases and demijohns of liquor, and headed back in the dead of night, unloading their haul in the mangroves of Saddle Bunch and Boca Chica keys. One night, loaded with five hundred cases of bootleg, *Runaway's* bottom fell out just as Lowe was easing into the thicket at Saddle Bunch. It took divers a week to recover the contraband.

Coast Guard cutters kept a steady patrol of the Florida Straits, and customs agents and hijackers dogged the rumrunners' every move. If the feds got too close, the runners tucked into a creek or mangrove thicket and dropped their load overboard, thereby assuring they would be ticketed only for running without lights. The runners planned to return in the morning to retrieve their contraband, but sometimes they were outsmarted by thieves known as "pelicans." These bootleg hijackers were so-called because they would wait until the rumrunners had gone and then they would dive down, bring up the load of booze, and steal it.

The feds caught Paul Lowe only once. When they tied a towline to his boat, Lowe doused his boat with liquor and then lit it on fire. "When tow line burnt [sic], I hopped overboard," Lowe said at his trial. But luckily, the judge enjoyed a little bootleg himself from time to time. The judge sentenced Lowe to a year in a federal prison in Atlanta plus a $1,000 fine. Then he promptly suspended Lowe's sentence to thirty days in a Miami jail.

Even when they caught the bootleggers red-handed and confiscated the booty, Prohibition enforcers often met with betrayal. A deputy U.S. marshal in Key West once seized forty-five-gallon demijohns of *aguardiente* (liquor), smuggled cargo that was off-loaded on Stock Island, and arrested the rumrunners. Too busy with the apprehension of the bootleggers to deal with the disposition of the demijohns, the marshal deputized a passerby, asking him to take the liquor to Fort Taylor and turn it over to the U.S. Army for safekeeping overnight.

The marshal booked the prisoners at the jailhouse. The next day, at a preliminary hearing before the U.S. commissioner, the marshal presented his evidence—forty demijohns filled with . . . water! Unbeknownst to the marshal, his new deputy happened to be the money man for a competing rumrunning ring. The quasi-deputy had gone home and emptied the *aguardiente* into his bathtub and refilled the demijohns with simple *agua*—water. Case dismissed!

The good old, bad old days of bootlegging in the Florida Keys faded into the musings of the two drinking buddies sitting under a lazily turning ceiling fan in a sawdust-carpeted bar. "You should change the name of this place," Hemingway urged Russell that historic December evening. The dive was now legal, respectable. At Hemingway's suggestion, Joe Russell renamed his establishment "Sloppy Joe's," in honor of the club the two friends frequented together during Prohibition in Havana. Sloppy Joe's is the oldest licensed bar in Florida.

MOTHER NATURE'S FURY

- 1935 -

SEPTEMBER 2, 1935. THE CLOCKS STOPPED at 8:00 p.m., and, for seventeen-year-old Bernard Russell, life as he knew it began to end.

The Russell clan had lived on Upper Matecumbe Key since 1854, when John Henry Russell, Bernard's grandfather, first farmed pineapples, then tomatoes and key limes, on a bayside homestead granted to him by President Franklin Pierce. By 1935, the growing dynasty numbered sixty members, all of whom lived in close proximity on a stretch of ocean beach astride the mighty Atlantic on the northern end of the island.

For young Bernard, life revolved around his immediate family— father John A. Russell, mother Catherine Louise, and his three sisters. He attended classes in a two-room schoolhouse with his cousins and children from the neighboring Pinder, Albury, and Parker families. Excitement consisted of watching Flagler's railroad train pull into the station twice a day with mail and supplies or meeting the ferry from Key West at night. Whenever he could steal a couple of hours away from his chores, he went fishing, reveling in the magic of the sun and the sea that defined his idyllic existence.

When, at the end of August, the radio's evening news forewarned a "big blow coming from the direction of the Bahamas," the Russells weren't overly concerned. Mother Nature regularly bestowed hurricanes upon the Florida Keys, so the family knew how to batten down and shutter up. During the next forty-eight hours, however, John Russell's barometer showed that the minimal hurricane had intensified significantly. By the middle of the afternoon on September 2, the family decided to evacuate their beach home and flee to the center of the island.

Bernard's aunt, uncle, five cousins, a family friend, and his immediate family hunkered down in the inland "hurricane house," as they did for other hurricanes. John Russell had built the structure as a packinghouse for his key lime harvest, fortifying the building to withstand hurricane-force winds and elevating it two and a half feet above ground to escape tidal surge.

The family lit gas lanterns and settled in to ride out the storm. Conditions continued to worsen. The wind howled and shrieked, the front door vibrated vehemently, and the walls pulsated as if they would implode. (The family had no way of knowing its velocity, but by this time winds had reached nearly two hundred miles per hour.)

Bernard leaned against the door in an effort to keep it from blowing off its hinges. Water sloshed across his feet. He dipped a finger into the muddy liquid and touched it to his lips. Taste buds confirmed his fears—salty! The sea seeped into their sanctuary, at first slowly, then with greater vengeance. Within minutes the sea would likely smash the "hurricane house" to bits and reclaim all who remained within.

John Russell made the most difficult decision of his life: He instructed each member of his family to hang on to another person, go outside into the storm before the wind and water demolished the house, and attempt to make it to the higher ground of the railroad station. It was 8:00 p.m.

Bernard grabbed his twenty-one-year-old sister, who in turn clutched her small child, and held them as tightly as he could. He hung onto the doorframe for a brief moment, feeling the house shake to its foundation, and summoned the courage to step into the inky darkness outside. This was the point of no return. Nothing prepared Bernard for the ferociousness of the storm. Tree limbs, roof pieces, and massive unidentified objects whizzed by his head. A racing river of water assaulted him. Within seconds, his charges were sucked from his arms, disappearing into the night. He caught a glimpse of his mother as the wind catapulted her into the howling beyond.

The forces of nature lifted Bernard and blew him into the lime groves. A piece of flying debris hit his back, knocking him facedown in the roiling water. For a time, the object remained atop his back, forcing him to gasp for breath in the crushing deluge. He thought, "This is it!" Suddenly, the rushing water dislodged the object and he staggered to his feet. The storm had rendered him impotent over his own destiny, so Bernard submitted to its overwhelming powers and went with the flow.

The water kept rising. Bernard felt lost in a black hole, alone in the universe. Bumping into a heap of trash, he climbed the five-foot mound in an attempt to find higher ground, but his foot got stuck in the wreckage. No amount of tugging or shaking would dislodge the appendage. His only hope was to keep his head above water, so he stood tall with his back to the wind, cupped his hands over his nose, and wrung breath by breath from the rain-saturated air.

The water, now up to his chin, miraculously receded a few feet. Bernard heard someone yelling. He wasn't alone after all! Working his foot free from the rubble, he crawled down the trash hill and through the darkness toward the disembodied voice, shouting as he went. To his surprise, he stumbled upon his father. Joyous and thankful for this unexpected discovery, the two clung to each other until daybreak.

First rays of dawn revealed paradise lost. The hurricane, still blowing hard, had literally leveled Matecumbe and stripped it naked. Tree stumps peppered the landscape, and only one of the island's sixty-one buildings remained standing. Bernard could see from the Gulf of Mexico to the Atlantic Ocean without obstruction. A ten-car Florida East Coast Railway Extension train, which had come down from Miami in a futile attempt to evacuate several hundred World War I veterans working on a federal highway project linking the mainland with Key West, had been washed off the tracks by the strong winds and storm surge. The locomotive languished on its side and boxcars lay tossed hundreds of feet from the grotesquely twisted train tracks.

Bernard and John wandered through hell in a daze. Hundreds of bodies lay strewn everywhere—drowned, crushed, impaled, decapitated—unrecognizable by their sandblasted faces. The two survivors took refuge in an overturned boxcar until the wind died down, but it took two days before emergency crews arrived from the mainland and Key West to offer any assistance.

The 1935 Labor Day hurricane, with winds gusting to 250 miles per hour and a seventeen-foot storm surge, demolished the entire Russell family compound. But the human toll it took reached an even more catastrophic level. Bernard's mother and siblings had perished, along with forty-five other members of the clan, thirty of whom were never found. Only eleven of the sixty had survived.

Flagler's $27-million railroad, totally destroyed, also died with the hurricane, never to be rebuilt. In all, the "Storm of the [twentieth] Century" claimed more than four hundred lives. Corpses of the victims, swollen and split open in the intense tropical heat following the storm, were cremated in four mass funeral pyres. Their ashes lie in rest in a stone crypt fronting an eighteen-foot-tall Keys limestone monument alongside U.S. Highway 1 in Islamorada. Carving on the simple hurricane memorial depicts the storm—palm trees bent in the wind amid curling waves—and is inscribed thusly: "Dedicated to the memory of the civilians and war veterans whose lives were lost in the hurricane of September second 1935."

And what became of the Russells? Descended from hardy Keys pioneer stock, the survivors rebuilt their homes and their lives. Bernard married his childhood friend, Laurette Pinder, who also lived through the deadly hurricane. Together they raised their family in Islamorada. Many a hurricane has touched the Florida Keys since 1935, and although Laurette headed for the mainland with the first blow every time, her husband never budged from the islands. Bernard figured he had already been to hell and back, his life mysteriously spared. Only by standing chin to chin with Mother Nature, he reasoned, would he ever find out why.

AGAINST ALL PROTOCOL

- 1943 -

July 18, 1943. Lieutenant Nelson G. Grills left Richmond Naval Air Station, near Miami, at 1900 hours, commandeering his K-ship zeppelin—K-74—southward along the Florida Keys toward the Florida Straits for its night combat patrol. K-74, a 252-foot-long envelope of cotton, synthetic neoprene, and paraffin that encased 456,000 cubic feet of helium, was part of a fleet of 135 such blimps guarding America's coasts during World War II. Carrying a crew of ten, the Goodyear-built blimp car was equipped with radio, radar, and sonar and was armed with four five-hundred-pound depth bombs and a .50 caliber machine gun.

Never intended for heavy combat, K-74 instead monitored convoys of American merchant ships traveling between the Gulf of Mexico and the Atlantic through the Florida Straits. Protocol dictated the airship should advise Navy warships or fighters of any German U-boat sightings but should not attack on its own. (U-boats proved a constant threat during the Battle of the Atlantic, sinking 574 merchant ships in

1942—twenty near Florida's shores alone.) Powered by two Pratt and Whitney R-1340 Wasp engines, the K-ship could reach a top speed of only seventy-seven miles per hour. But, because the blimp could hover indefinitely, it could force a U-boat to stay submerged for hours.

From K-74's station above the Florida Straits, Lieutenant Grills and copilot John Jandrowitz monitored two merchant ships making their way through the Straits. At 2340 hours, radiomen Robert Bourne and Jerald Giddings spotted a third blip on the radar screen. Grills ordered navigator Darnley Eversley to move the K-ship closer. At five hundred feet, Grills spotted a wake. There, heading 220 degrees north at fifteen to eighteen knots, on a direct course toward the two American ships, was a German U-boat. The sub, U-134, was running on the surface, charging its batteries. (When a German U-boat dove, it had to switch from diesel power to electric power, which reduced both its speed and its effectiveness.) Much of the U-boat's crew was on deck.

Grills determined the sub was closing in on the merchant ships too rapidly to follow normal protocol. Instead, he ordered mechanic Jonathan Schmidt, bombardier Isadore Stessel, gunner Garnet Eckert, seaman John Kowalski, and the rest of the crew to battle stations. Staying within the cloud cover, Grills circled over the sub widely and positioned the blimp for attack. Petty Officer Eckert climbed into the gun berth overhead and held his fire until ordered. Petty Officer Stessel squatted at the bombsight window. Grills throttled up to top speed, dropped altitude to 250 feet, and commenced a bombing run on the U-134.

Just then, the U-boat's captain, Hans-Günther Brosin, spotted K-74, and the sub began firing its deck gun at the blimp. Airship gunner Eckert returned fire. An incoming round hit the airship's Plexiglas windshield. U-134 then turned portside so K-74 would find a narrower target. Antiaircraft fire hit the airship again, causing its starboard engine enclosure to begin sparking and smoking. The airship's rpm dropped suddenly, and the blimp began to drift. Eckert, using an entire belt of ammunition, reloaded and kept firing. Bullets ricocheted off U-134's deck.

Gunfire from the sub became sporadic and then mysteriously ceased altogether for a time. The blimp was now nearly directly over the sub, in point-blank range. Pilot Grills ordered, "Bombs away!" at the precise moment U-134 resumed anti-aircraft fire. Gunfire hit K-74 dead on. Spinning out of control, the airship stood on its tail, nose to the heavens and shot up to one thousand feet. The cabin began to shudder severely, throwing the crew about the airship. Then K-74 flipped over.

Pilot Grills jettisoned the two 380-pound outboard fuel tanks in an attempt to regain control of the airship. The blimp stabilized horizontally, momentarily. Leaning out the engine service hatch with a fire extinguisher, mechanic Schmidt dampened the fire in the starboard engine. But antiaircraft fire had peppered the airship's envelope and shot away the rudder and tail elevators. Pilot Grills could no longer control K-74. The airship began descending, tail first.

Throwing everything they could out of the blimp in a desperate attempt to stay aloft, the crew prepared for an emergency landing at sea. Radioman Bourne managed to send out a coded mayday message sixteen times before K-74's tail touched the water and the blimp began to sink. Radioman Rice looked at his watch: 2357 hours.

As Grills tossed classified information into the sea and gave orders to abandon ship, the U-boat, which sustained serious damage and could not submerge, limped off into the night. The airship's crew threw out their life raft but mistakenly tossed the tether line as well, causing the raft to immediately inflate and float away. The men hastily donned life jackets and scrambled out of the sinking blimp control car into the sea.

Unaware that the sub had left and concerned about imminent capture by the Germans, Grills ventured back inside the dark, partially submerged control car to retrieve a pistol he kept stashed under his seat. Unable to retrace his steps in the darkness, Grills mistakenly exited on the opposite side of the car from his crew. The current immediately swept him away. Drifting farther and farther from the airship, Grills decided to swim toward the Florida Keys, which he judged to be about twenty nautical miles away.

Meanwhile, the rest of the crew hung onto the sinking airship, its envelope slowly deflating into giant folds. Isadore Stessel had cut his leg and punctured two of his life jacket's air pockets on the bulkhead when he jumped out of the control car. Unable to swim, he thrashed about in the sea, frequently swallowing salt water. Jandrowitz urged Stessel to grab the airship's tailfins and pull himself partially out of the water, just as he, Eversley, Bourne, and Rice were doing. Eckert, Schmidt, Giddings, and Kowalski, thinking the Germans may still return to the airship, chose to swim away from the blimp. The wind and current divided the men into two groups and carried them about one thousand yards apart.

Another airship in the fleet, K-32, deciphering Bourne's coded mayday, alerted Richmond Naval Station, then headed to assist K-74. The closest ship in the area, USS *Dahlgren*—an old four-pipe destroyer from World War I presently serving as a training ship for the Navy sonar school in Key West—got up to steam and left Mallory Dock at 0300 hours.

A Coast Guard seaplane sighted the huge oil slick surrounding the sinking blimp at 0745 hours but, having removed its life raft to accommodate political observers from Key West, the plane could offer no immediate assistance. Instead, it buzzed the nine sailors below and radioed the *Dahlgren,* still fifteen nautical miles away, with the exact location of the survivors.

K-74 sunk at 0800, abandoning its crew to the mercy of the sea. High waves threatened to further break up the groups of survivors. Isadore Stessel, his leg bleeding and life preserver partially deflated, couldn't keep up with the others. He had drifted some fifty feet from his crewmates when they spotted a shark making a beeline for the bombardier. Suddenly, Stessel disappeared under the water, only to reappear with a bloody head and shoulders and an agonized expression. Then the shark pulled him under again. Stessel never resurfaced. Sharks circled the other crewmen but did not attack.

USS *Dahlgren* arrived at 0945 hours, pulling alongside the survivors and scattering the sharks with rifle and submachine-gun fire. The vessel's whaleboat picked up the eight surviving men and took them to the *Dahlgren*. Bourne was treated for first-degree fuel burns on his back and chest. The whaleboat retrieved an empty life jacket—probably Stessel's—about two thousand yards away.

Two Coast Guard patrol crafts, the destroyer USS *Reuben James*, two Navy sub-chasers, and airships K-46 and K-32 joined the *Dahlgren* to search for missing pilot Nelson Grills and to look for the German U-boat. Just as dusk settled in on July 19, K-32's rear lookout, Petty Officer Max May, spotted Grills about two thousand yards away. *Subchaser* 657 and *Dahlgren's* whaleboat, with a medical officer onboard, sped to the rescue. Grills, still alive but delirious, dehydrated, and sunburned, had swum more than twelve miles from the rescue point before losing his stamina. He had been in the water for nineteen hours. Sharks accompanied him for much of his ordeal but they never attacked him.

The altercation between U-134 and K-74 was unique: Never before had a German submarine and a U.S. Navy blimp engaged in battle. Furthermore, in more than five hundred thousand airship surveillance hours, K-74 was the only blimp lost in combat. Grills and the crew of K-74, initially in trouble with the Navy for not following protocol, were vindicated in 1961 when German records of the incident were closely analyzed. The U.S. Navy granted all the men commendations (Isadore Stessel posthumously) and Grills received the Distinguished Flying Cross twenty years after the event. Stessel remains the only U.S. Navy airshipman ever killed in enemy action. And, U-134? Two British Royal Navy bombers sunk the submarine off the coast of Spain in August 1943, as it was en route to France for repairs.

ISLAND AT WAR

- 1962 -

OCTOBER 22, 1962. PRESIDENT JOHN F. KENNEDY INTERRUPTED prime-time radio and television programming at 7:00 p.m. on this autumn Sunday evening, to alert the American public that the Soviet Union had installed medium- and intermediate-range offensive ballistic missiles in Cuba, a mere ninety miles from the United States' southernmost point. The president pledged that our nation would stand eyeball to eyeball with the Soviets until the weapons, capable of reaching the United States, were removed. He also announced a naval quarantine, or blockade, of Cuba, to stop the flow of arms from the USSR. Meanwhile, covert preparations for air strikes on Cuban missile sites and a possible all-out invasion were underway, posthaste.

We were a nation on the brink of war—conceivably World War III. The president's announcement on October 22 shocked most everyone in the nation except the residents of the Florida Keys, who, perched on the front lines, had been privy to the secret for more than a week. Key West, only five minutes from Havana by jet fighter, had been tapped to become the leading player in the largest short-term mobilization of men and equipment to date, since World War II. As a crucial U.S. military base, the southernmost city became the focal point of the confrontation for the duration of the Cuban Missile Crisis.

Four days before President Kennedy declared the Cuban blockade, a troop transport deposited five thousand Marines in Key West, and fourteen Navy F4B Phantoms landed at Boca Chica Naval Air Station. The U.S. Army stealthily erected radar installations on Grassy and Sugarloaf Keys.

On October 20, the Federal Aviation Administration began building a new control tower at Key West International Airport, a facility futilely sought after by Key West officials for more than three years. Completed in warp speed, especially by government standards, the tower was fully operational in two days, at which time the Navy cancelled all leave for Key West personnel and placed them on high alert.

Military rations and ammunition, including napalm, rolled south, as a constant stream of mostly Army vehicles oozed down U.S. Highway 1. An Army Hawk surface-to-air missile battalion convoy, moving overland from Maryland to Key West, was stopped by a Virginia state trooper for exceeding the designated weight limit. Unable to reveal its secret mission, the unit meekly accepted a ticket from the officer and moved on.

The Army leased Key West's Wicker Field (a city-owned ball park surrounded by a ten-foot-high concrete-block wall), for $1.00 a year to use as a vehicle and troop staging area. (Locals suspected the area might be used as a prison camp should an invasion occur.) The military also took over the one-mile-long Smathers Beach for its radar and missile launching area. They dug foxholes, filled sandbags, and strung barbed wire along South Roosevelt Boulevard. The Army mounted missiles on launchers on the beach, aiming them at Cuba, but less knowledgeable about the ocean than the Navy, they had to make a mad dash to save their weapons the first time high tide came in.

By noon on October 22, thirteen submarines, five destroyers, and three destroyer escorts stationed in Key West steamed out to sea. A mere fifteen minutes before President Kennedy's message to the American public, the Pentagon contacted the Association of American Railroads, requesting 375 flatcars to move air-defense and air-warning units to Florida.

At the precise moment the president addressed the nation that evening, U.S. jet fighters thundered out of Boca Chica into the moonless night, an "airborne alert" precautionary measure taken in case the commander-in-chief's words triggered offensive action by Cuba and the Soviet Union. As the president was speaking, Secretary of Defense Robert McNamara placed the entire U.S. military establishment on DefCon 3 (defense condition) status. That night, Key West did not sleep.

As day dawned on October 23, the standoff continued and so did U.S. preparation for invasion. Scores of Air Force and Navy pilots arrived in Key West, billeted in local hotels and resorts, such as the Holiday Inn, the 167-room Casa Marina, and the Key Wester Resort. (Uniformed military personnel increased from three thousand to twelve thousand in three days.) Dozens of fighter jets and medium bombers screamed into Boca Chica Naval Station, clogging its runways with a virtual parking lot of aircraft. The military took over control of Key West International Airport and reassigned Monroe County sheriff's deputies as control tower guards. A Texas First Armored Division conducted beach landing exercises on Sugarloaf Key. Military patrols searched for bombs or signs of sabotage on the water pipelines and bridges along US 1.

The Joint Chiefs of Staff put the U.S. military on Defcon 2 status (the level just before all-out war) on October 24. Our nation would be ready to attack Cuba or the USSR or both in a matter of days. Air Force RF-101 Voodoos flew tree-level photoreconnaissance missions over Cuba. America panicked, invading grocery stores and stocking bomb shelters for a possible nuclear attack.

But, in spite of the fact that one small megaton bomb dropped in the center of Key West would make a 300-foot-deep, one-and-a-half-mile-long, and half-mile-wide hole, decimating virtually everything and everyone on the island, life in Key West remained curiously, quintessentially laid back. Islanders hunkered down, but they did not overreact. After all, October in the Florida Keys, the height of hurricane season, had always been fraught with a degree of danger. "Where can you go that you're going to be protected, always safe?" said one resident. "We'll take our chances with our own."

Civil Defense officials warned residents that any alerts issued henceforth would be the real thing—an attack, not a drill. Sheriff and fire departments cancelled employee time off, and guards policed electric power and communications centers around the clock. School in much of the Keys went on as usual, although most military families in Key West immediately pulled their children out of classes and evacuated the island. Most residents took the military buildup in stride—parking along the beach, watching military maneuvers, taking photographs, and chatting with the military. Locals joked that the barbed wire had been installed at Smathers Beach, not to protect the troops from the Cubans, but to ward off the flock of Key West chicks flirting with the military.

On October 27, now forever referred to as "Black Saturday," the Soviets, in an apparent escalation of the crisis, fired an SA-2 surface-to-air missile (SAM), shooting down a U-2 reconnaissance plane and killing its pilot, Major Rudolf Anderson. Key West and the world held its breath, and with good reason. U.S. military policy (Contingency Plan No. 312, agreed to by President Kennedy) determined that any Cuban SAM site that shot down an American U-2 was to be neutralized within two hours. Sixteen F-100 Super Sabre fighter jets stood armed and ready on thirty-minute alert at Homestead Air Force Base at the top of the Keys. The general in charge, LeMay, had already given readying orders to the F-100s when he received a call from the White House, instructing him to rescind his directive and to proceed only on direct command from the president of the United States. The order never came.

President Kennedy decided, instead, to issue an ultimatum to the Soviets: Commit to remove the missiles by the next day, October 28, or the United States would remove them by force. Premier Nikita Khrushchev blinked, and via an open letter from Khrushchev to Kennedy, read over Radio Moscow by the president's deadline, the Soviet government ordered the dismantling of the missile bases and the return of all equipment to the USSR.

President Kennedy's official announcement on November 2, that the Soviet missile bases in Cuba were in the process of being dismantled, elicited a collective sigh of relief from the American public, especially in the Florida Keys. The commander-in-chief visited the Key West military complex on November 26 to offer the nation's profound gratitude. "We are very much indebted to you all," President Kennedy told the troops.

And although the residents of Key West nonchalantly went about their business during the Cuban Missile Crisis, the dashing young president's three-hour visit sparked quite another reaction from the local population: They turned out in droves, clapping and cheering in the narrow streets that stretched from Boca Chica Naval Air Station to the downtown Navy surface and submarine base, the route President Kennedy took, riding in a red convertible almost close enough to touch.

Only one nonmilitary Key West citizen met officially with the president that day, however: Key West mayor C. B. Harvey presented President Kennedy with a bent golden key to the city. "The key is bent as a symbol of the strain which the Cuban missile crisis has put on the Key West economy," Harvey cheekily stated with typical Florida Keys irreverence for all things official. President Kennedy replied with characteristic class and dignity: "I certainly realize that and I hope my visit here will help things."

FLOTILLA TO FREEDOM

- 1980 -

APRIL 1, 1980. HÉCTOR SANYÚSTIZ STOMPED THE gas pedal of the "borrowed" bus to the floor, jostling his three companions. Full speed ahead, he crashed his vehicle through the gates of the Peruvian Embassy in Havana, Cuba, in a desperate attempt to secure political asylum from Fidel Castro's Communist regime. Cuban government guards opened fire, wounding the thirty-one-year-old unemployed bus driver and his passengers. In the ensuing confusion, one guard was killed.

Castro demanded that the Peruvians turn over the gatecrashers, but the embassy refused. In a fit of pique, Castro removed all Cuban guards from the embassy, leaving it vulnerable and unprotected. Within thirty-six hours, 10,856 Cubans stormed the embassy, also seeking asylum. Héctor Sanyústiz had just triggered a human tsunami that would ultimately flood the U.S. city of Key West—ninety miles south, across the Florida Straits—for more than five months.

In actuality, Cuban leader Fidel Castro may have sparked the tidal wave himself in 1979, when he released three thousand political prisoners from government custody and subsequently allowed one hundred and ten thousand exiles to return to Cuba for weeklong visits with their families. Because they'd abandoned the revolution, these people had previously been referred to as *gusanos,* a term meaning worms or caterpillars. With their lives positively transformed by exile, however, they soon were lauded as *mariposas,* or butterflies, because their visits brought money and consumer goods to the languishing island nation.

The familial visits had an unsettling effect on the Cuban populace, however, germinating long dormant seeds of unrest. Held under Castro's thumb in a restrictive Communist regime for decades, growing numbers of Cubans desired escape at any cost. Desperately, they sought asylum in foreign embassies or hijacked boats and fled to neighboring countries.

The hordes of asylum seekers camping on the embassy grounds trampled the spring flowers and ate leaves off the trees. It was rumored that they even killed the ambassador's cat and cooked and consumed it. The international press was all over the story. Castro had inadvertently created a public relations nightmare for himself: Cubans would rather eat cats and tree leaves than live in Communist Cuba!

Castro needed a plan to get rid of the dissidents. He engaged Napoleón Vilaboa, a Miami car salesman and Bay of Pigs veteran who sought release of that conflict's prisoners still held by the regime, to help him arrange for exiles to come to Cuba by boat, pick up a load of embassy malcontents, and take them to the United States. In return for each boatload carried away, the exile could take one relative out of Cuba.

Vilaboa began blasting his message over a Spanish-speaking Miami radio station on April 11, beseeching all exiles to beg, borrow or buy a boat—twenty feet or more—and follow him to Cuba, forming a flotilla to freedom for their compatriots. On April 19, Vilaboa, aboard his boat, *Ochún,* led a convoy of forty-two vessels to the Cuban Port of Mariel. The waterborne exodus, dubbed the Mariel Boatlift, officially began.

Day dawned quietly in Key West the next day, April 20; the last of the spring breakers had headed north. Buoyed by Vilaboa's news that Castro would allow relatives of exiles to leave Cuba, Diego Galván and a couple of other Key West exiles wasted no time readying two private lobster boats—the *Dos Hermanos* and the *Blanchie III*—and sailed for Havana ahead of Vilaboa's flotilla. The Cuban border patrol led the Cuban-Americans to the Port of Mariel, and, inspecting their list of relatives, allowed five to leave, along with thirty-seven embassy dissidents. The forty-two refugees, seasick but exultant, docked in Key West on Monday, April 21, the first wave of a human hurricane that would hit the city broadside in the coming days.

The tsunami gained momentum on Tuesday. The thirty-nine-foot *El Mir* arrived in Stock Island, just north of Key West, bringing four family members and twenty-six refugees from the Peruvian embassy. *Big Baby,* a sixty-seven-foot fishing boat, left Mariel at 4:00 p.m. with 202 refugees on board. The sixty-foot vessel *Tote,* fully loaded, followed closely behind. The U.S. Coast Guard air patrol sighted fifty vessels sailing out of Key West and an equal number between Miami and Fowey Rocks, all headed south to Cuba.

Word reached South Florida on Wednesday, April 23, that Castro now would allow anyone who sailed to Cuba to bring back as many relatives as they wanted, without having to take any of the embassy dissidents. The rumor spread, in Havana and in South Florida, like a tropical heat wave. Telephone calls to Key West numbered fourteen thousand. Within hours, a constant stream of boats on trailers snaked down U.S. Highway 1, from Miami to Key West, where they lined up fifty to a hundred deep in a two-mile circle around Key West's charter-boat dock, waiting a turn to be launched. In Cuba, long lines of automobiles stretched from Havana to the Port of Mariel, where occupants waited as hours turned into days, in hopes of snagging a seat aboard one of the freedom fleet's vessels.

The exodus began spiraling out of control on April 24, with reports that even Cubans without relatives in the United States could leave, if they could find a way to the Port of Mariel and could secure passage on one of the vessels. President Carter declared the freedom fleet illegal and threatened to prosecute boat owners who participated in bringing Cuban refugees to Florida. The warnings went unheeded and unenforced.

Pandemonium ensued at boatyards in South Florida and the Keys, as potential buyers tried to outbid each other. Cuban-Americans, desperate to pick up waiting family members, competed with entrepreneurs hoping to make a quick buck by charging the frantically fleeing refugees $1,000 to $3,000 a head. Capitalism collided with supply and demand, and the freedom flotilla morphed into a freedom-for-a-price fleet.

The refugee flotilla became an armada—one boat in sight of another in a ninety-mile trail through the Mariel–Key West corridor. As many as two thousand vessels, which ranged from eighteen to ninety feet in length, peppered the Florida Straits, sailing continuous loops between Cuba and Key West. (A good percentage of the boats—small pleasure or fishing craft—would have had a difficult time traveling the five miles to the reef, let alone crossing the Straits to Cuba.)

The boats deposited refugees—hundreds at a time—on the concrete pier of Truman Annex, from where they were taken to a condemned former U.S. Navy warehouse that had no bathrooms, no water, and no electricity. Here the refugees received food and dry clothing and were granted a ninety-day parole visa. Then they began the long wait for transportation north, by bus or plane, to Miami, Eglin Air Force Base, or other designated processing centers.

"On Sunday, April 27, at about one o'clock, the weather went to hell—a mini hurricane passed through," noted a Coast Guard observer. Cutters, helicopters, and planes searched the dozens of abandoned and overturned boats in the waters of the Florida Straits for victims (two victims were found). More than two hundred boats waited out the storm in Key West harbor on Monday. Another four hundred lined up for launching. The Cuban government reported seventeen hundred vessels sat in the Port of Mariel, awaiting departure.

Nearly twenty-two thousand refugees swamped Key West during the third week of the sealift, which showed no signs of abating. More than fifteen hundred boats packed Mariel; more than seventy-five thousand refugees waited in line for safe passage out of Cuba. Key West nearly reached its breaking point. Florida governor Bob Graham declared Dade and Monroe counties disaster areas. Additional Coast Guard troops were sent to Key West, later relieved by a contingent of U.S. Marines. One hundred additional border control agents headed to the southernmost city.

On May 14, the Carter administration finally set forth a comprehensive national policy regarding the Mariel boatlift. Previously Carter had pledged "an open heart and open arms" for the Cubans. But the mass exodus had taken on a life of its own: Larger and larger vessels were making passage, grossly overloaded, and no end was in sight. More than forty-one thousand refugees had already been processed.

The president announced a five-point program designed to bring order and safety to the mass immigration. Carter ordered all boats to return from Mariel without passengers or they would face heavy fines, vessel seizure, and possibly criminal prosecution. He proposed a government boat- or airlift instead.

Fidel Castro, however, refused to play ball. Cuban gunboats blocked the Mariel harbor exit, refusing to let the fourteen hundred vessels already anchored there to leave Cuba without a load of refugees. The sealift continued.

By June 3, more than a hundred thousand refugees had entered Key West harbor, but the flood slowed to a trickle by mid-month. The flotilla to freedom did not officially end until September 26, when Fidel Castro unceremoniously pulled the plug and, without preamble, closed the Port of Mariel.

More than five thousand vessels carried one hundred twenty-five thousand Cuban refugees to Key West in the five months of the exodus, forever known as the Mariel boatlift. Most of these immigrants settled in Miami and beyond, but many remained in the Florida Keys, where they have become integral threads in the islands' rich fabric of humanity.

IF AT FIRST YOU DON'T SECEDE . . .

- 1982 -

APRIL 23, 1982. THE PEOPLE OF THE FLORIDA KEYS had been hopping mad for nearly a week. On April 18, at about 3:30 p.m., the United States Border Patrol and the Drug Enforcement Administration established an unprecedented roadblock checkpoint on U.S. Highway 1, at the top of the Keys, directly across from the Last Chance saloon in Florida City. The feds meticulously searched all vehicles leaving the islands, reportedly looking for undocumented aliens and illegal drugs. This being the only road in or out of the Keys, the action snarled traffic all the way back to Key Largo. Travelers, trapped in their cars for hours on the desolate, uninhabited "eighteen-mile stretch" without so much as a gas station or a convenience store, became frustrated and angry.

The roadblock continued twenty-four-hours a day, every day, paralyzing the Keys and threatening to choke off the islands' lifeblood—tourism. A media circus ensued. Press helicopters filmed overhead, televising the ongoing event on the national evening news.

Every illegal alien and drug smuggler in the Western world must have known about the checkpoint.

When an injunction filed by Key West attorney David Horan against the government—citing unreasonable search and seizure—failed to permanently eliminate the checkpoint (random checks were to continue indefinitely), community leaders took matters into their own hands and invoked more desperate measures. At exactly noon on Friday, April 23, the Florida Keys symbolically seceded from the Union, proclaiming itself "The Conch Republic," and promptly declared war on the United States.

Seven hundred cheering Key West citizens and flabbergasted tourists watched as Key West mayor Dennis Wardlow, standing on the back of a flatbed truck in Key West's Clinton Square, hoisted a distinctive ocean-blue flag adorned with a flaming gold sun and a pink conch shell, and read "The Conch Republic Proclamation of Secession":

> *We, the people of Key West, are called Conchs. Sometimes we are called Conchs with affection, sometimes with humor, and sometimes with derision.*
>
> *I proclaim that Key West shall now be known as the Conch Republic and, as the flag of our new republic is raised, I hereby state to Washington and the rest of the United States, and the world, what the Conchs are and were.*
>
> *When Jamestown, Virginia, was settled by Englishmen who were fed up with the arrogance, the derision, the abuse of rights by a despot, a king without compassion or sense of humanity, another group was settling in the Bahamas and they were called 'Conchs.'*

They were known as Conchs because they hoisted flags with the tough, hard conch shellfish on them, indicating they'd rather eat conch than pay the king's taxes and live under his tyranny.

There's our flag. It has a conch on it. We secede from the United States. We've raised our flag, given our notice, and named our new government.

We serve notice on the government in Washington to remove the roadblock or get ready to put up a permanent border to a new foreign land.

We as people may have suffered in the past, but we have no intention of suffering in the future at the hands of fools and bureaucrats.

We're not going to beg, to beseech the nation of the United States for help. We're not going to ask for something we should naturally have as citizens, simple equality.

If we are not equal, we'll get out. It's as simple as that.

The first step was, like Mariel [Mariel Boatlift, 1980], up to Washington. This step is up to us.

We call upon other people of the Florida Keys to join us or not, as they see fit. We're not a fearful people. We're not a group to cringe and whimper when Washington cracks the whip with contempt and unconcern.

We're Conchs and we've had enough. We're happy to secede today with some humor. But there's some anger, too.

*Big trouble has started in much smaller places
than this.*

*I am calling on all my fellow citizens here in the
Conch Republic to stand together, lest we fall apart;
fall from fear, from a lack of courage, intimidation by
an uncaring government whose actions show it has
grown too big to care for people on a small island.*

Long live the Conch Republic!

Proclaiming himself Prime Minister of the Conch Republic,
Wardlow introduced the Minister of Defense, City Commissioner
Joe Balbotin, who fired the first shot. Using the Conch Republic's
weapon of choice—hard, stale Cuban bread—Balbotin hit a cooper-
ative young uniformed naval officer over the head, then immediately
handed over the loaf and surrendered.

The mock rebellion ended just minutes after it began. Prime
Minister Wardlow announced the Republic would now apply to the
United Nations for $1 billion in foreign aid and war relief to rebuild
the island nation. The secession made newspaper headlines across the
United States.

The roadblock simply disappeared without apology or explana-
tion, unceremoniously dismantled one night in June 1982. But the
Conch Republic, one of the greatest public relations stunts of all
time, soon attained legendary status. The nation created a mock navy
and air force and issued blue-and-gold passports, inscribed with the
motto: "We have seceded where others failed."

The Republic's self-appointed Postmaster General, Pasquale
Goicoeches of Key Largo, issued a set of four aqua- and flamingo-
colored commemorative stamps, deemed worthless by the U.S. Post
Office but considered attractive envelope dressing by the new nation.

And in 1994, two original tunes became the Republic's official songs: "The Conch Rebellion," by Bobby Green, became the Republic's battle hymn, and "Conch Republic," by MeriLynn and Joe Britz, its national anthem.

The hype didn't end with a song, however. Key lime pie, conch fritters, and conch chowder became national foods. The hibiscus was voted its national flower. And a disagreement on the national bird— the frigate bird or the pelican—rages to this day.

The Conch Republic is a state of mind, and Key West never misses a chance to burnish its image. An "official" delegation crashed the 1994 Summit of the Americas in Miami, attracting massive media coverage and giving government officials a few laughs along with more than a few headaches.

In 1995 during the federal government budget crisis shutdown, the Conch Republic, stating that the temporary closure of the Dry Tortugas National Park was costing tour operators $30,000 a day in lost revenue, unsuccessfully attempted to pay the park manager $1,600 a day from private funds to reopen. When the bribery failed, overzealous officials threatened to use three antique biplanes loaded with stale Cuban bread to bomb the park's Fort Jefferson.

The U.S. Army Reserve 478th Civil Affairs Battalion came to Key West in September 1996 for training exercises simulating a geo-graphically isolated foreign nation. The Conch Republic took mock personal offense, claiming the Army had not consulted with the island government about the exercise. The Republic convened its war cabinet at the Schooner Wharf Bar and planned to attack the Reserves with humor and respect. Working round the clock, the Republic's munitions factory, La Dichosa Bakery, began grinding out stale Cuban bread.

Before the "deadly" confrontation, however, Army Major Muller conceded to the Republic's faxed demands. More than two hundred of Key West's hardiest partiers lined the streets as the Army troops made their way onto the Stock Island Bridge. Conch Republic Supreme Commander of the Armed Forces "Admiral" Wilhelmina Harvey (84-year-old former mayor of Key West) stopped the lead vehicle and demanded Major Kim Hooper request permission to cross over the bridge and onto the island nation. He complied, and with the welcoming blast of a conch trumpet, the Army was invited to enter the Conch Republic.

Every year Key West celebrates Conch Republic Independence Day by throwing a ten-day party around April 23. Food, foolishness, and frivolities permeate the annual celebration blowout, but the highlight is always a mock sea battle between the Conch Republic "Navy" and the U.S. Coast Guard. Boats of every size and shape take on government vessels in Key West Harbor for the biggest water fight in history. Onlookers pelt both sides with stale Cuban bread and rotten vegetables. Although impossible to tell who wins the annual battle, the Conch Republic's popular foreign policy—"The Mitigation of World Tension through the Exercise of Humor"—continues to rule the day.

FINDERS, KEEPERS

- 1985 -

July 20, 1985. "WZG9605. Unit 1, this is Unit 11," Kane Fisher shouted into the crackling marine radio of his rusting tugboat, *Dauntless.* "Put away the charts," the six-foot, six-inch redhead thundered to his father, Mel, back in the Key West office of their company, Treasure Salvors, Inc. "We've got the mother lode!"

For sixteen years, sixty-two-year-old Mel Fisher had been telling family, friends, investors, impatient creditors, and strangers on the street: "Today's the day!" And finally, through sheer perseverance and faith in his intuition and knowledge, Fisher and company's day had arrived at last. At 1:30 p.m., Mel's youngest son Kane and his crew discovered the elusive main ballast of the Spanish galleon, *Nuestra Señora de Atocha,* which had sunk with seven sister ships during a hurricane on September 4, 1622, near the Marquesas Keys, about forty-one miles west of Key West.

Headed for Spain via Cuba with its fleet, the *Atocha* was loaded with $400 million in treasure from Mexico and Central America:

twenty-four tons of silver bullion, 180,000 pesos of silver coins, 582 copper ingots, 125 gold bars and discs, 350 chests of indigo, 525 bales of tobacco, twenty bronze cannons, and 1,200 pounds of silverware. The ship also carried thirty-eight members of Spanish nobility and aristocracy and their valuable belongings as well as an undisclosed amount of treasure smuggled aboard in order to avoid Spanish taxation.

For Mel Fisher, the dream of finding buried treasure began when he read Robert Louis Stevenson's *Treasure Island* as a child in Glen Park, Indiana. By age eleven, he had fashioned a hard-hat diving outfit to explore a muddy lagoon near his home. His aspiration persisted through college at Purdue University, a stint in the U.S. Army during World War II, and relocations to Chicago and Colorado. While raising chickens with his parents in Torrance, California, in 1950, Mel opened his first dive shop in a feed shed on his property and met the girl who would share his dream.

Mel sealed his fate when he married Dolores Horton in 1953: The couple spent their honeymoon diving shipwrecks in the Florida Keys and became hooked on underwater exploration for life. Four children and fifteen years later, the Fishers moved to the Florida Keys. The Fisher kids could scuba dive before most of their peers could ride a bicycle. It was 1968. The search for the *Atocha* had begun.

Mel and his divers first concentrated their efforts in the Islamorada area in lower Matecumbe, believing stated legends that the *Atocha* had sunk in the *"Cabeza de los Martires Matecumbe."* Finding no traces of the ship, Mel consulted historian Gene Lyon, who was researching shipwrecks in Spain. Lyon agreed to check *Atocha's* original records. The result: The 1622 fleet went down near *Cayos de Marques,* today known as the Marquesas Keys, west of Key West. The reason for the confusion was simple: Spain considered all the Florida

Keys as the Matecumbes. Mel moved his operation to Key West and began exploring the waters surrounding the Marquesas.

Mel Fisher invented a specialized tool called a prop-wash deflector, or "mailbox," which his dive tugboats used in their treasure-hunting endeavors. He fitted huge elbow-shaped metal tubes over the salvage ship's propellers. The force of the propellers directed a high-pressure stream of water to the sea bottom, creating holes twenty to thirty feet in diameter and three to five feet in depth. With silt and sand cleared away, any buried treasure below was revealed. (Maintaining that the procedure destroyed marine resources by blowing craters in the sea bottom, U.S. District Judge Edward Davis ordered Mel Fisher to stop salvaging with mailboxes in July 1992.)

The search for the *Atocha* proved a roller-coaster ride for the Fisher entourage. Setbacks offset discoveries. Despair dampened elation. On July 20, 1973, when Kane Fisher was only sixteen years old, tragedy struck the expedition. Mel Fisher and his family paid the ultimate price. The salvage tugboat *Northwind* took on water in the middle of the night while its crew was sleeping. The boat capsized and quickly sank, trapping and drowning Mel and Dolores Fisher's eldest son Dirk, his wife Angel, and diver Rick Gage. Racked with grief but knowing that finding the *Atocha* was Dirk's dream as much as their own, the treasure hunters persevered.

The sea bottom terrain changed with every storm in the centuries since the *Atocha* met its watery grave. As the wooden ship deteriorated, tides and currents scattered its treasure. Treasure Salvors found enough artifacts, coins, and clues over the ensuing years to narrow their scope of exploration to a sixty-square-mile area.

Some of the dive fleet explored a quicksand area known as the Bank of Spain, forty-one miles off Key West, uncovering occasional finds of gold, emeralds, and artifacts. Kane Fisher believed the mother lode of treasure was in deeper water and doggedly followed a ten-mile scatter line of ballast stones in Hawk Channel instead. The *Dauntless* searched the area, called Kane's Trail, ballast stone by ballast stone for two and a half years without finding any treasure. (Ballast stones were put in a ship's hull to steady them.)

On July 17, 1985, Captain Kane Fisher's spirits soared when *Dauntless's* magnetometer and sonar both revealed a large mass on the sea bottom southeast of the tug's usual target area. Divers wasted no time descending the depths. Silver coins, copper ingots, and ballast stones littered the sea bottom. The next day revealed a cache of silverware. This could be the jackpot.

Encouraged that the day they'd all been waiting for was finally near, Mel Fisher motored out to the *Dauntless* on July 19, to assist Kane in taking sonar readings to determine the best sites for the next day's exploration. Together they decided on a spot two hundred feet in front of the boat. Mel headed back to Key West for the night.

Saturday, July 20, dawned hot and sultry, without even a sea breeze. A storm was brewing to the south. Kane anchored the *Dauntless* over the predetermined spot and blasted the site with his mailboxes. Andy Matroci and Greg Wareham dove down to the crater the mailboxes had carved in the sand. Visibility was good—almost thirty feet. Andy spotted a mound of silver coins and went over to investigate. Greg, metal detector in hand, swam toward what looked like a long, low reef of gray rocks, crawling with spiny lobsters and tropical fish.

As he approached the reef, the metal detector crackled to life. "This mound is not coral," Greg thought. Suddenly he spied the timbers of a ship's hull and signaled to Andy. They had stumbled upon the main ballast of the *Atocha*. They had found the treasure. Grabbing each other in a bear hug, the two men cavorted like porpoises then sped to the surface. Andy broke through the water first. "It's here! He shouted to the crew of the *Dauntless*. "It's the main pile! We're sitting on the silver bars."

For Mel Fisher, his family, and the "golden crew," as they now were dubbed, today was definitely the day. However, their jubilation was bittersweet. It was ten years to the day that Dirk and Angel Fisher had lost their lives in the search for the *Atocha*. "I did it for Mel," Kane said, referring to his father. "I just wanted to make Mel's quest come true, because of everything that happened. I had to give him my best to make it happen. Plus for my brother, too, because I know he wanted us to go on. It [the quest for the gold] brought us closer [as a family]. It made us happy and a lot of other people too."

"Kane kept saying, 'It's in the mud,'" Mel Fisher said. "I believed him. It's like when you put the last piece in a jigsaw puzzle," said Mel Fisher. "It's fantabulous. Fantabulous!"

From the five-foot wall of *Atocha*'s main ballast, divers brought up treasure worth hundreds of millions of dollars and preserved priceless archaeological information of the Spanish colonial era. By noon on July 26, they had recovered seven unmarked treasure chests, each filled with about three thousand silver coins (coins were worth from $200 to $12,000, depending upon their condition). By 1:30 p.m., they found a smaller wooden box, metal hinges miraculously intact, filled with gold bars. In mid-August in the silt next to the wreck, Kane's crew found seventy-six more gold bars, weighing more than 150 pounds.

Three computer operators spent a year cataloging *Atocha*'s treasure. About six hundred investors and employees shared the booty, which was divvied up and distributed on October 16, 1986. Employees were stunned at what they received: Salvage captain Robert LeClaire started diving for Mel Fisher in 1978 for $50 a week. He received the third largest emerald—64.5 carats—valued at $200,000. "It really blew me away. Maybe Sears will give me a credit card now," LeClaire joked.

Mel Fisher always claimed the search for the *Atocha* was about the hunt, about solving the puzzle, not about the money. Nevertheless, Fisher battled the state of Florida in 113 federal court cases and one U.S. Supreme Court case to keep the treasure. He emerged victorious from each case, allowed to keep the bounty under the "finders, keepers law." (Those who spend their own money in the pursuit of treasure, get to keep it under the rules of free enterprise.) Mel Fisher personally received a 4 percent share of the treasure, which included two of the priceless coin-filled wooden chests.

Mel Fisher died in December 1998 after a long illness, requesting that his ashes be scattered over Kane's Trail, his treasure path to the end of the rainbow. His dream, however, continues. Nearly fifteen years to the day of the discovery of the mother lode, Mel's middle son, Kim Fisher, and his dive teams discovered *Atocha*'s treasure-filled sterncastle, the rear structure in which the Spanish nobility, aristocracy, and clergy—and their considerable valuables— were housed.

The search goes on . . . and on . . . and on.

THE PREZ AND GREY'S GHOSTS

- 1989 -

JANUARY 13, 1989. CROWDS OF LOCAL RESIDENTS CLUNG to the chain-link fence at the edge of Marathon Airport's only runway, eyes peeled for a glimpse of the expected important visitor. Scores of reporters infested the tiny terminal, pacing like thoroughbreds at the starting gate of a big race.

Air Force Two touched down smoothly and on schedule. Vice President George H.W. Bush stepped from the aircraft with a wave. This was the last weekend before his inauguration as America's forty-first president, and he looked forward to a few days of total relaxation and fishing in the Florida Keys, one of his favorite angling destinations.

Preparations for his visit had reached manic proportions by Keys standards. Fire marshals closely inspected the secluded Tarpon Flats condominium, owned by Joe Hudson and Tim Hixon, where Mr. Bush planned to stay. Secret service agents scoured every inch of Cheeca Lodge, at which the president-elect would dine, even combing the golf course and examining the drainpipes. Mr. Bush's staff commandeered hotel rooms, and the news media took over all Cheeca Lodge's conference suites for use as pressrooms, hooking up extra phones and copy machines.

The sixty journalists of the White House press corps had requested a press conference upon his arrival. Mr. Bush didn't relish a sparring match about the influx of Nicaraguans to Miami or about problems within the Reagan administration's Justice Department, but he agreed to a brief question-and-answer session and tried to keep it light. "This is part of my work experience," he told reporters. "Because it is here I will get new ideas, creative clearing the mind of the underbrush. [sic] I'll be able to think anew."

Asked about bonefishing, Mr. Bush demonstrated his casting technique and said: "It's like hunting. You see them [the fish] coming up with their tails in the air, noses in the mud, then you see the mud turning up. A guide way up on a platform on the back of a flat, shallow-draft boat spots the mud [turning up]. Be very still. They try to get in front of them . . . The most it takes is three minutes for the whole operation . . . Shallow water, flat. They're hard to get [the bonefish]. If we don't get any of them, we'll go up some river and go for snook. It's all catch-and-release . . ." With that, the president-elect escaped to his limousine and sped off with his motorcade to Islamorada for a rendezvous with the gray ghosts.

Mr. Bush had stalked the gray ghosts, as the wily bonefish of the flats are called, on four other occasions in the Florida Keys, each time guided by his friend, George Hommell, owner of World Wide Sportsman fishing emporium. But this time, as president-elect, Mr. Bush resigned himself to the fact that fifteen boats carrying secret service agents and security forces from the U.S. Coast Guard, the Florida Marine Patrol, U.S. Customs, and the Everglades National Park Service, as well as overhead helicopter patrols, would shadow his every move, a restriction that would probably give the evasive fish the edge. Mr. Bush knew he couldn't make the fish bite, but he loved being out on the water under any circumstances.

Several hours later, however, aboard a seventeen-foot flatsboat named *Backlash,* using an eight-pound test line on a Shakespeare spin-cast rod, Mr. Bush launched a live shrimp at a school of fifteen bone-fish George Hummel had spotted from the poling platform. A thirteen-pound ghost hit his bait and screamed 150 yards into the shallows on its first run. The president-elect prevailed, catching—then releasing—the bonefish, which was reportedly within three pounds of the world record. "Pound for pound, it's the fightingest fish that there is anywhere in the world," Mr. Bush later told reporters.

Mr. Bush considers himself a fishing conservationist, whose angling philosophy was shared by author/angler Zane Grey, first president of the Long Key Fishing Club, in 1917. Considered the pioneer of Florida Keys fishing, Grey convinced railroad magnate Henry Flagler to convert the construction camp used to build the Long Key portion of the Florida Keys East Coast Railway Extension into an elite sportfishing camp. Attracting notables and million-aires, the compound nestled in a coconut grove and accommodated seventy-five anglers. The camp included a main lodge building, four-teen cottages, a post office, general store, and an elaborate railroad depot, all connected by wooden boardwalks over the sand.

The cardinal rule of the Long Key Fishing Club, and the basis of catch-and-release fishing supported by Mr. Bush and others, is to repress the wholesale killing of fish. A sign in the lodge flatly stated: "Good sportsmanship does not consist in a big catch, but in the use of light tackle with a reasonable catch. To preserve the species and to keep the place what it is today, the best spot in Florida for big game fish, it is suggested that the sportsman should limit himself to two. . . . Any fish caught above that number should be returned to the water."

An insatiable angler, Zane Grey painted vivid word pictures of his fishing escapades in the Florida Keys. He believed his responsibility as a writer was to convince his readers of the importance of preserving the world's gamefish. Grey considered bonefish anglers a special breed, calling them the "Bonefish Brigade." Like George H. W. Bush, Grey loved the hunt and catch of the elusive, ghostlike gray fish, which he described as "the wisest, shyest, wariest, strangest fish" he had ever encountered. "The cunning of the fish was baffling; the bite almost imperceptible, and tactics used by this fish beyond conjecture," Grey recounted.

The Labor Day Hurricane destroyed the Long Key Fishing Club in 1935, but the principles of catch-and-release fishing established there became the code of honor in the Florida Keys. Zane Grey and George Herbert Walker Bush never tipped a rod together, but their shared interest in stalking the gray ghosts ensured them a commingled legacy in Islamorada. Zane Grey is immortalized with pictures and memorabilia in his namesake lounge atop World Wide Sportsman. Photos of former president Bush's fishing accomplishments, which continued throughout his presidency and beyond, grace the walls of Cheeca Lodge.

DROWNING THE *AFRICAN QUEEN*

- 1992 -

MAY 15, 1992. THE SHUTTER-HAPPY TOURIST—infamous and luckily anonymous—leaned out of moviedom's grand old lady, trying to capture a better camera angle. Blissfully unaware, she tripped the steam launch's mechanical boatlift switch and inadvertently played a leading part in the fate of the famed *African Queen*.

With more reincarnations than a B-movie star, the *African Queen* had performed many roles before starring in the tourist scene at the Holiday Inn docks in Key Largo in 1992. Fabricated by the British East African Railway Company in 1912, then shipped to Uganda and assembled, the thirty-foot tramp steamer provided jungle transport in the African swamps around Lake Victoria and Lake Albert for decades. Simply constructed with a steel hull, brass boiler, and mahogany trim, the *Queen* labored in mundane transport until, like an actress-wannabe, she was fortuitously discovered by a famous American movie director.

In 1951, James Agee, John Huston, and Peter Viertel adapted C.S. Forester's 1935 novel *The African Queen* into a screenplay that would become a Hollywood classic starring Humphrey Bogart and Katharine Hepburn. Produced by Sam Spiegel and directed by Huston, many of the movie's scenes were filmed in central Africa. Integral to its plot was a wood-fired tramp steamer, the *African Queen,* which traveled through the backwaters of the Ulanga River, negotiating swamps and rapids, to reach Lake Victoria during World War I, when the lake served as a battleground for rival British and German colonial forces.

Huston's research staff found three British-built steamers still traversing Lake Victoria and arranged with the governments of Uganda, Kenya, and Tanzania to use the boats for the duration of the film shoot. Distillate engines, which ran on anything from kerosene to gin, powered these boats, so the engines of the steamers had to be dummied up with wood and papier-mâché to replicate the fictional *African Queen.* Production crews rigged one steamer for interior shots and one for waterline shots, creating the illusion of deteriorating wooden launches. The third steamer functioned as a back-up boat, usually ferrying supplies around the floating set.

After the movie wrapped in 1952, all three *Queen*s left their fairytale movie turn and returned to reality, again providing barge service in Lake Victoria. Fifteen years later, in 1967, the tramp steamers went on the auction block. San Francisco restaurateur Fred Reeves, after reading a Foreign News Service notice of the impending auction, flew to Nairobi, Kenya, to bid on an *African Queen.* When he arrived he found the boats had already been auctioned off. Undeterred, he contacted a plantation owner who had purchased one of the movie vessels for $400 and offered him $750 and a replacement boat. The deal done, Reeves shipped his *African Queen* seven thousand miles, aboard a merchant ship, back to San Francisco.

Reeves refurbished the *African Queen,* restoring her big-screen splendor, and used the craft as a dry-dock attraction at charity fund-raising events for several years. *Queen* changed ownership several times until, in 1970, boating and collecting enthusiast Hal Bailey of Eugene, Oregon, purchased her. Determined to make the tramp cruise the waters again, Bailey spent two years researching steam engines at the University of Oregon library, refitting the steamer with a boiler he scrounged from a Willamette Valley nursery and a circa 1903 engine that formerly operated in a local applesauce cannery.

"I searched the world for parts and equipment," Bailey said of his quest to outfit the *African Queen* like a real-life operating version of the movie creation, down to the most-minute detail. Bailey set out to find two wooden cases of Gordon's gin, which were stowed onboard the *Queen* when Charlie Allnut, the boat's fictional gin-loving Cockney mechanic, and Rose Sayer (Katharine Hepburn) embarked on their adventure. By chance, the English company found two of the discontinued cases in an old warehouse and shipped the empty crates to Oregon. Bailey fashioned the cases into seats for the boat.

Makeover complete, the *African Queen* was reborn. Drawing only four feet of water, the thirty-by-eight-foot, flat-bottom steel boat, now powered by 125 pounds of wood-fired boiler pressure, glided along Oregon's Sun River, mahogany trim gleaming. "It's been very satisfying," stated Bailey. "When she's fired up, and the fly-wheel's turning, with oil pumps spurting, smoke coming out of the stack, k'chunk-k'chunking down the river, and I give a blast on the whistle, well . . ."

But in 1975, Hal Bailey inexplicitly put the tramp steamer in dry docks at his newly purchased Ocala, Florida, ranch. Her hull full of leaves and spiders in her boiler, the *Queen* languished until 1981, when the owner of the Key Largo Holiday Inn, Jim Hendricks, a retired Kentucky lawyer, offered her a comeback role. Purchasing the

African Queen for $65,000, Hendricks docked the boat in a canal bordering his resort. "So many people associate Key Largo with Bogie. What would be a more natural home for the *African Queen*?" asked Hendricks.

Restoring *Queen* to her former weather-worn, movie-set glory once again, Hendricks repowered the vessel to burn thirty to forty bats of charcoal, instead of wood, for each outing. Hendricks toured the boat all over the country. During ensuing years she participated in steamboat races, she starred at the World Fair in New Orleans, and she escorted Queen Elizabeth of England and her yacht *Britannia* into the Kingston, Ontario, harbor during that city's two hundredth anniversary celebration.

On May 15, 1992, however, the *African Queen* was docked at home port alongside the Holiday Inn Resort in Key Largo, hosting droves of visiting Bogart and Hepburn fans, when the aforementioned overzealous photo-snapper inadvertently tripped the switch that lifts the boat out of the water onto davits each evening. The mechanical boatlift slowly crept up, catching the bow and pivoting the vessel on the line that tethered it to the dock. The *Queen* quickly filled with water and sank to the bottom of the canal, whiffs of smoke still curling from her smokestack.

According to Hendricks, this wasn't the first time the *African Queen* sank. During the movie filming in Africa in 1951, the boat was tied up on the bank of the Ruiki River. A local man had been engaged to guard the boat each night. One morning, producers arriving at the set discovered the steamer missing. Upon inquiry, the guard pointed to the river. Asked why he didn't save the sinking vessel, the man replied that he had only been hired to *watch* the boat.

While it took five days in Africa to get the sunken boat up and running, Hendricks and the crew of Blackbeard Towing and Salvage, utilizing a crane, raised the *Queen* from the depths in a matter of hours. Since the simple vessel sported no electronics, which could be water damaged, she only needed to be pumped dry, rinsed off, and loaded with fresh charcoal. On May 17, she was good to go.

And go, go, go she has, ever since. Hendricks has exhibited the *African Queen* around the world, but most often she is home, in Key Largo, evoking memories of Bogie and Kate and still graciously accommodating her admirers.

A TALE OF TRUE LIES

- 1993 -

NOVEMBER 18–NOVEMBER 29, 1993. THINGS ARE NOT ALWAYS as they seem. Helen Tasker led a ho-hum life with her ho-hum computer salesman husband Harry. Or so it seemed. Now she sits in the back of a black limousine barreling up the Overseas Highway in the Florida Keys, held captive at gunpoint by a female terrorist from the Iranian Crimson Jihad. Harry is probably dead after a fiery shootout and explosion only minutes ago at a terrorist camp on a nearby unin-habited island. The terrorists have nuclear warheads they plan to transport by truck to destroy four American cities. And she's lost her shoes. What's a girl to do?

Grab the gun, kill the limo driver, and smack her captor over the head—twice—with a champagne bottle, it appears. Then find a way to get the hell out of the car, which by now, driverless, is careening out of control between the guardrails of the Old Seven Mile Bridge. Harrier jets scream overhead, shooting missiles and blowing up the nuclear weapon-filled trucks, not to mention a huge segment of the bridge.

Two government helicopters close in on the limo. Helen opens the roof window to see Harry, miraculously perched on the copter's running blade, holding out his hand to her. Harry, it turns out, is actually a spy and has been for more than fifteen years, their entire married life. Hanging by one leg and one arm from the helicopter, Harry tries in vain to grasp Helen's outstretched arm. The car crashes against the railing, throwing Helen in a heap on the roof of the car. The Taskers connect at the very second the limo sails off the bridge. The car crashes into the watery depths below, and a screaming Helen, clasping Harry's arm in a death grip, flies through the air like a trapeze artist without a safety net.

"Cut! That's a wrap!" yells director James Cameron, as the Harrier jets and helicopters land on the Marathon side of the Old Seven Mile Bridge.

This day, at least, things definitely were not as they seemed.

In reality, the city of Marathon braced itself as the Lighthouse Production Company invaded the Middle Keys for two weeks of filming the action-adventure comedy, *True Lies,* starring Arnold Schwarzenegger and Jamie Lee Curtis as Harry and Helen Tasker. To live in a real, live movie set, locals had to endure some inconveniences, such as several explosion-filled nights, intermittent bridge closings, and a ten-day banishment from Moser Channel, the deep-water boat passage between Florida Bay and the Atlantic Ocean. But for most residents, it was an exciting fortnight.

Local Joshua Rosenblatt never imagined himself training to be a terrorist. Although he is a Jewish American, his dark features, firearms experience, and the fact he can speak fluent Farsi—the native tongue of Iran—won him a small role as an Iranian Muslim terrorist in the movie. Producers transformed a remote area of Sugarloaf Key into a terrorist-camp set for the movie scene in which Harry and the terrorists fight an explosion-filled night battle.

Thirty-one-year-old Uzi Gal, a national judo champion and former high-ranking officer in the Israeli Special Forces, transformed Rosenblatt and a group of other extras—college students, models, waiters, even an accountant—into frighteningly believable terrorists. Exacting a rigorous workout regimen from the recruits at the Duval Square Health and Fitness Center in Key West, he said, "I feel like I have a whole army to train and command, but terrorists are actually kind of small people. All it really takes is motivation."

Three McDonnell Douglas AV-8B Harrier Jump Jets of Marine Attack Squadron 223, nicknamed "the bull dogs" (on loan from the Department of Defense for a mere $2,410 per hour) practiced for days before filming the high-speed strafing runs along the Old Seven Mile Bridge. Because of safety concerns for motorists during the Harrier jet "attacks," traffic traveling along the Seven Mile Bridge, which runs parallel to the old bridge, experienced intermittent five- to fifteen-minute stoppages, up to fifteen times a day. For the most part, motorists sat through the action with good humor. With front-row seats and real-time surround-sound special effects, the stranded drivers were entertained and fed: Production company employees handed out soft drinks and hot dogs as well as bumper stickers that proclaimed: "I was held hostage on the Seven Mile Bridge during the filming of *True Lies*."

In the movie, the Harrier jets were called in to blow up the center span of the Old Seven Mile Bridge, so that the terrorists could not make it to Miami with their trucks full of nuclear warheads and threaten the United States with nuclear holocaust. This center span was removed in 1982 when the new Seven Mile Bridge was completed, so a local engineering firm was called upon to create a temporary truss for the missing span near Pigeon Key, fashioning it to look like the rest of the bridge. When the Harriers fired their missiles, the center span of the bridge blew up. Or did it?

Actually, the missiles were edited into the movie, and the bridge did not really blow up at all. A scale model, one-fifth the size of the actual four hundred-foot center span was constructed of balsa wood and breakaway materials on Sugarloaf Key. The eighty-foot miniature bridge was blown up at a later time to simulate the attack, and the footage was edited into the movie to create the image of the exploding bridge.

For subsequent scenes, to maintain the impression that part of the bridge was destroyed, two barges were submerged across the width of Moser Channel under the Old Seven Mile Bridge. Blocks and pieces of the old Twenty-Second Avenue Bridge in Miami were loaded onto the barges to simulate the shattered remains and debris of the blown-up bridge. The sunken barges, under twenty-four-hour guard by the Florida Marine Patrol, were lit up like Christmas trees at night so that local boaters wouldn't hit them.

Stuntman Billy Lucas drove one of the terrorist trucks to the edge of the blown-up bridge for a scene where the truck teeters precariously but doesn't fall over . . . immediately. The prop truck hung over the edge of the bridge for several days of filming, noticeable to all motorists traveling over the adjacent Seven Mile Bridge. In the movie, a pelican flies over and sits on the hood of the truck, throwing it off balance and causing it to plunge dramatically into the sea. In reality, the production crew pushed the truck off the bridge as the cameras rolled.

And what about Helen? Did she really hang by a hand over the ocean? A stunt woman performed the most dangerous parts of the sequence, but director James Cameron convinced Jamie Lee Curtis to perform the final stunt herself. "Will you be up there with me?" she asked. He replied that he'd be hanging out of the helicopter shooting the scene himself. So, on November 22, her thirty-fifth birthday, as Helen dangled from a wire a hundred feet off the ocean, with nothing but water and sea creatures beneath her, Jamie Lee Curtis's blood-curdling shrieks could be heard for a mile. Some things, even in the movies, are exactly as they seem.

ON HER SIDE

- 2002 -

MAY 17, 2002. AFTER EIGHT YEARS OF meticulous planning and preparation, twenty-eight thousand hours of cleaning, and $1.25 million, Murphy's Law trumped the game before it began. Just hours before her scheduled reincarnation as an artificial reef in the Florida Keys National Marine Sanctuary, the U.S.S *Spiegel Grove* prematurely sank of her own accord, twisting onto her side, capsizing, and ending up with her bow sticking partially out of the water.

The 510-foot retired U.S. Navy landing ship dock (LSD 32) had enjoyed a distinguished thirty-three-year military career before being decommissioned in 1989 and sent to join the rusting, aging vessels of the "mothball fleet" in James River, Virginia. Commissioned in 1956 and named for the Fremont, Ohio, estate of nineteenth president Rutherford B. Hayes, the *Spiegel Grove* transported U.S. troops and amphibious landing vessels—called "fast squadrons"—to aid friendly governments worldwide during the Cold War conflict with the Soviet Union.

Nicknamed the *Spiegel Beagle* (the image of Charles Schultz's cartoon character Snoopy, riding an alligator under the name "Top Dog," was painted on the ship's floor), *Spiegel Grove* delivered medical supplies to Dr. Albert Schweitzer's leprosy clinic in Lambaréné (now in Gabon), Africa, in the 1960s. She served as one of the emergency rescue vessels during Commander Scott Carpenter's 1962 splashdown of the second U.S. orbital space flight *Aurora 7*, and she stood by at *Apollo 14*'s reentry near the Samoa Islands in the South Pacific in 1971. Involved with the evacuation of Americans from an escalating civil war in Beirut, Lebanon, in 1976, and called into service during the American invasion of Grenada in 1983, *Spiegel Grove* managed to escape enemy attack for her entire career.

So when in July 1994, leaders of the Key Largo dive community decided to adopt a decommissioned ship from the U.S. Maritime Administration's James River Reserve Fleet (MARAD) and sink her six miles offshore the Florida Keys, it was only fitting that a ship of *Spiegel Grove*'s pedigree be chosen. *Spiegel Grove* was slated to be the largest ship in the world ever to be intentionally sunk as an artificial reef.

Fundraising ensued, U.S. Environmental Protection Agency standards set, and by late 1999, ownership transferred to the state of Florida. Readying the ship to be sunk in an environmentally protected area proved a monumental task that consumed hundreds of thousands of dollars and took years to complete. Ten-man teams from Bay Bridge Enterprises in Chesapeake, Virginia, disengaged more than four hundred thousand linear feet of cable; flushed oils, gases, and fluids from 110 fuel tanks into tanker trucks; and removed electronics, vent gaskets, insulation, ductwork, refrigeration units, and any other equipment that might contain polychlorinated biphenyls (PCBs) that would poison fish and other marine organisms. To ensure diver safety and prevent possible entrapment, workers welded hatches and doors either open or shut, and cut holes in the ship's body chambers for easier passage.

Before *Spiegel Grove* could be scuttled, however, a group of five organizations and government agencies had to inspect the ship and sign off: Environmental Protection Agency, Florida Keys National Marine Sanctuary, U.S. Coast Guard, Florida Fish and Wildlife Conservation Commission, and Monroe County. Finally, on May 8, 2002, with the official go-ahead received just two days earlier from the U.S. Coast Guard, the 6,880-ton *Spiegel Grove* was towed from Virginia to Key Largo for her long-awaited renaissance.

As it unexpectedly sunk that fateful Friday in May, *Spiegel Grove* proved the old adage that the best-laid plans can, indeed, run amuck. Resolve Towing and Salvage of Fort Lauderdale wasted no time addressing the ship's reorientation conundrum. The world watched as salvage vessel *Lana Rose* pulled alongside *Spiegel Grove* on May 22, to begin the arduous task of rolling the eighty-four-foot-wide ship onto its side, even repositioning it upright, if possible. Using underwater torches, technical divers cut holes in the sides of the ship and attached giant dive-lift bags, into which they pumped air. By June 6, nearly seventy such airlift bags were installed, capable of adding five hundred tons of buoyancy to the ship.

On June 9, tethered to *Spiegel Grove*'s upside-down hull with cables, two tugboats began their Herculean effort to roll the ship over. Working around-the-clock, the tugs finally rolled the vessel onto its starboard side, and it slipped beneath the sea. At 6:35 p.m. on June 10, 2002, divers confirmed that the ship had finally been "valet parked" on its side on the ocean floor, in 130 feet of water near Dixie Shoals.

On June 24, after resolving an unexpected fluid leak and installing ten mooring buoys for dive-boat tie-offs, officials invited the public to dive *Spiegel Grove* for the first time. They projected that over a period of decades, coralline algae would grow on the hull of the sunken ship, fostering development of a coral ecosystem akin to that living on the natural coral reef.

In its first submerged year, divers weren't the only curious creatures exploring the ship. *Spiegel Grove* attracted more than 125 species of fish, including a resident goliath grouper. The well deck—170 feet long, 45 feet wide, and 40 feet deep—once used for military landing craft, and a helicopter platform equipped with two fifty-ton swivel cranes, dominate the ship's stern. The ship itself is like a gigantic, ghostly museum. Nearly as long as two football fields, its cavernous interior hides a labyrinth of chambers that once sheltered a small village of troops.

Spiegel Grove, the most infamous botched scuttling in Florida Keys history, languished on her starboard side for more than three years, while northeast currents dredged a trough underneath the vessel. Then Mother Nature decided to take matters into her own hands and balance the scales: Outer wind bands of Hurricane Dennis brushed the Florida Keys on June 9, 2006, producing twenty-foot-high waves and pulsing strong currents throughout the reef.

Exploring the Dixie Shoals two days later, diver Bob Snyder couldn't believe his eyes—amid a mirage of churned up silt stood the 510-foot *Spiegel Grove,* as massively upright as a mountain. Dennis had finished the job! And, enduring two more hurricanes later in the season—Rita and Wilma—the ship never budged, proving another old adage: "Don't mess with Mother Nature!"

RUFFLED FEATHERS

- 2004 -

FEBRUARY 15, 2004. ARMANDO PARRA SNIPPED HIS last lock of the day, then closed the door on the Conch Town Barbershop on Fleming Street, where he had cut hair for the past forty-five years. Tonight marked the end of the first week of a new part-time venture for the sixty-three-year-old, third-generation Conch. He changed into a pair of old shorts, donned a work shirt emblazoned with the words, "Key West Chicken Catcher," hopped into his two-toned blue van, and set off through the streets of Key West in search of his next victim.

The city of Key West had a poultry problem—a big poultry problem. More than two thousand wild hens and roosters aimlessly wandered the two-mile by four-mile island with reckless abandon. The birds ran down the middle of tourist-clogged Duval Street, went into the post office and other government buildings, and entered popular restaurants—on their feet, not on a plate. The chickens even attended mass—more than once—at St. Mary Star of the Sea Catholic Church, arrogantly marching right down the aisle to the altar.

Roosters routinely crowed at the slightest provocation—the full moon, a car's headlights, not to mention the first rays of dawn. Hens hijacked private gardens, scratching and tearing up flowerbeds and vegetable plots. Chicks frequented city playgrounds. All together, the fowl fouled Key West's beaches, where they defecated all over the sand and spiked the water's bacteria count with fecal matter to the point that the areas sometimes had to be closed to the public.

A storm of complaints washed through the bureaucracy of the Key West City Commission, but the birds had reason to be cocky: They had enjoyed the run of the southernmost city for nearly seventy-five years. From the early days of Key West, right through the Depression, every household owned chickens, essential for eggs and protein. Cuban immigrants bred prize-winning roosters for their Sunday afternoon cock fights. By the mid-twentieth century, how-ever, cock fighting was outlawed in Key West, and grocery stores sold prepackaged, ready-to-eat poultry. People released their chickens to forage on their own.

Free-ranging through the streets of Key West, the hens and roost-ers reproduced at a rapid pace. (A hen can lay a dozen eggs at a time, which only take twenty-nine days to hatch.) The birds had no natu-ral predators in the island city: The only foxes and wolves in Key West were of the human variety, and the birds could be so mean that even the island cats wanted nothing to do with them. Furthermore, the chickens had the law on their side. A city ordinance declared it unlawful for any person to hunt, trap, shoot, seize, molest, or tease the birds. (Officials enacted the law to counteract voodoo practices by early Jamaican immigrants.)

Although Key West's native chickens had their critics and detrac-tors, about half the city's human population and virtually all the tourists loved the feathery creatures, regarding them as part of the island's charm. So it surprised no one that the Commission's relocation scheme to reduce the passel of pesky poultry—particularly the rowdy roosters—by hiring an official chicken-catcher, ignited a long-simmering local controversy.

Appointed by City Manager Julio Avael to function as an avifaunal bounty hunter, Armando Parra was contracted to capture—but not kill—one thousand chickens by September 30, for which he would be paid $20 per chicken. He was uniquely qualified for the job: His family had raised chickens for more than fifty years, and many of his relatives had bred fighting cocks when the gaming was still legal. Forbidden from harming the birds in any way, Parra was instructed to take the captured birds to Indigenous Park, on Stock Island, and place them in a large holding pen. Here the chickens would await transfer to a four hundred-acre South Florida chicken farm—described with public-relations pomp by government officials as a "Garden of Eden for chickens"—where the birds would idyllically live out their lives. (When a film crew from the University of South Florida checked out the address, however, they instead found a slaughterhouse.)

Armando Parra hunted Key West chickens every afternoon after one o'clock and all day on Mondays. By the end of the first eight days, he had captured fifty-seven truant chickens. The task was not easy. The chickens were extremely wild, and tourists complicated his mission by feeding the birds that congregated around his baited traps. The chickens, sated on popcorn and potato chips, often sauntered right past his enticements.

The barber's new profession provoked Key West chicken lovers to mutiny. The pro-chicken lobby accused government officials of being in bed with Colonel Sanders. They predicted an epidemic of cockroaches, scorpions, and ants if the birds were removed from city streets, advocating a chicken park or sanctuary instead of the perceived genocide.

Inspired and abetted by the self-proclaimed "Chicken Lady of Key West," Katha Sheehan, owner of the Chicken Store, a passionate poultry posse vandalized Parra's cages, releasing the ensnared chickens. Local chicken advocates, dubbed the Rooster Rescue Team, offered to pay Sheehan $20 per bird to find the gypsy chicks a new home. Now in open competition with Armando Parra, Sheehan packaged up the roosters and hens and mailed them to people around the United States who promised to keep them as pets.

By July, his roundup sabotaged at every turn by chicken sympathizers, Parra had captured only five hundred birds. Frustrated and disillusioned, Parra resented the city telling him which chickens he was supposed to catch. The city fathers were not pleased with his progress. Concluding that Parra had no chance of fulfilling his contract by the end of September, they summarily fired the Key West chicken-catcher. Chicken lovers rejoiced!

One would surmise that this ended the chicken wars. Not so! By early 2007, the victorious chicken population of Key West had soared to more than three thousand, and a new cadre of city officials began to obsess about a possible outbreak of avian flu sometime in the not too distant future. No incidents of the epidemic have been found in the United States to date, but the ever forward-thinking government "suits," aware that Key West is on the migratory bird path, envisioned a doomsday scenario in which migratory birds infect Key West chickens and kill the southernmost city's booming tourist industry.

Intent on hatching a comprehensive avian influenza plan, city commissioners are contemplating every alternative, from bringing back a chicken-catcher to feeding the birds birth control pills. Maybe it is time to put a chicken in every pot!

MAROONED IN MARATHON

- 2005 -

MARCH 2, 2005. CUBAN IMMIGRANTS HAD WASHED ashore for decades in the Florida Keys, but the mass stranding off Marathon this fateful Wednesday afternoon caught residents by surprise. Sixty-eight rough-toothed dolphins *(Steno bredanensis)*, which normally inhabit the deep offshore waters of the Gulf of Mexico and the Atlantic Ocean, marooned themselves, for no apparent reason, on oceanside flats and sandbars during low tide in scant inches of water. And thus began—about a quarter-mile off Key Vaca, between 74th and 89th Streets—the largest rehabilitation of stranded marine mammals in history.

Volunteers from the Southeast Regional Stranding Network and professional marine mammal experts, clad in wetsuits, rushed to the scene and formed rescue teams. They raced against time to move the dolphins into the deeper water of canals at the end of 66th and 88th Streets before the mammals expired. Frightened and disoriented, the gentle dolphins—most six to seven feet in length—squeaked and whistled to each other, communicating their distress.

A cold front complicated the rescue workers' assessment and stabilization efforts. Both the air temperature and the water in the canals were unseasonably cold. Standing in frigid water all night long, volunteers held the ailing dolphins' blowholes above water so that they could breathe. Hypothermia threatened dolphins and rescuers alike.

By March 5, thirty-six dolphins had died on the beach or in the water, but the remaining mammals were stable enough to be transferred to rehabilitation facilities. A refrigerated truck (donated by the Publix supermarket chain) transported the dolphins, load by load, to three marine mammal centers: Marine Mammal Conservancy (MMC) in Key Largo (twenty-six), Marine Animal Rescue Society (MARS) near Miami (two), and Mote Marine Laboratory's satellite in Summerland Key (four).

MMC maintained the largest operation of the three facilities. Their twenty-six dolphins survived the first night, all stable but still in critical condition. Twenty-four were in a lagoon sea pen, and a mother and calf stayed in an above-the-ground pool. The dolphins were numbered for identification. Caregivers fed the mammals fish gruel, and, to combat dehydration, the dolphins received Pedialyte and water via throat tubes. Veterinarians injected shots of vitamin E to help eliminate muscle cramping.

The weaker mammals still needed their blowholes held out of the water round the clock. Like mothers with sick babies, volunteers "walked" the dolphins around the medical pool, while the stronger survivors freely swam under their own steam. The first patients succumbed mid-morning on March 6. Within a week, survivors numbered only fourteen. A team of veterinarians conducted blood tests and medical assessments on the remaining dolphins.

National Marine Fisheries Service experts conducted necropsies on the dead mammals in search of the causes of the stranding and the ensuing deaths of the marine mammals. Three theories prevailed: Most commonly, marine mammals have long been known to strand when sick, injured, or disoriented. Too weak to survive in the depths, they head for the shallows to keep their blowholes above water so they won't drown. This, however, was the fourth rough-toothed dolphin stranding since July 2004, raising the possibility that something significant might have happened to change the species' environment or habitat.

Strangely and coincidentally, one day before the dolphin stranding, the USS *Philadephia*—a nuclear-powered submarine based in Groton, Connecticut—conducted training exercises with the Navy SEALS off Key West, about forty-five miles from Marathon. The submarine used the Navy's new Low Frequency Active (LFA) 235-decibel sonar, emitting underwater sounds equivalent to that of a commercial jet aircraft on take-off. These sounds could be heard beneath the sea as far as three hundred miles.

Marine mammals rely on sound waves for their very existence, from foraging for food to finding a mate. Scientists believe that sonar such as the LFA could frighten or disorient marine mammals, causing them to swim to the surface too rapidly. This rapid surfacing could cause sudden decompression, similar to what some divers experience as "the bends." If ascent from underwater depths is too fast, nitrogen bubbles form in body tissues, causing blood vessels to hemorrhage.

While the scientific search for a definitive cause of the stranding progressed, the dolphins' fight for survival continued at MMC and the other rehabilitation facilities. By the end of March, only a dozen rough-toothed dolphins were still alive at MMC. (The dolphins are called this because their teeth have vertical, wrinkly ridges). Eight swam freely, fluke-slapping and breaching in the deepwater lagoon. Three adults, which were monitored more closely, showed definite signs of improvement. And a juvenile calf called "the youngster," was still being bottle fed and remained in the basin.

Though MMC subsequently lost one more dolphin, the facility gained MOTE's sole survivor, a female, on April 12. The mammals voraciously ate capelin, squid, and herring that had been stuffed with vitamins and medication, and they actively cavorted in the lagoon. Toward the end of the month, seven dolphins were well enough to have their medications discontinued. The staff made plans to release them into the wild.

Meanwhile, on April 20, the MARS facility in Key Biscayne released its two rehabilitated dolphins—named Notch and Naia. Both nearly nine feet long and 350 to 400 pounds, the two rough-tooths were slid onto stretchers, covered with protective foam padding, and removed from the pool in which they had lived for seven weeks. Then, loaded side by side in the back of a pick-up truck, the dolphins took a short ride to the Coast Guard vessel *Reward,* clicking and squeaking to each other all the way. Two hours later, in four- to six-foot seas, amid fifteen-knot winds, seven miles offshore, Notch—fitted with a satellite tracking device on his dorsal fin—and then Naia, slid into the sea. Reuniting under water, the two swam away from the boat, near the surface, for about ten minutes, then dove and disappeared.

On May 3, in history's largest simultaneous release to date, amid pomp and media, MMC released five females and two males back into their native environment. All were fitted with VHF tracking transmitters and two also had satellite transmitters. (The devices were designed to fall off automatically in about six weeks.) The seven dolphins were placed on stretchers and taken by truck, with a Fish and Wildlife official escort, to two forty-five-foot Corinthian dive-boat catamarans, where they were loaded aboard—one dolphin, on a backboard, at each of the boats' seven exit points—and transported fourteen miles offshore Key Largo.

On the count of three, volunteers simultaneously upended all seven backboards. With a mighty splash, the dolphins swished into the six hundred-foot-deep sea. The mammals breached, then reassembled into a pod, and swam away. A tracking helicopter spotted the dolphins an hour later, hunting a school of fish. Together, the magnificent seven, as they were dubbed, traveled five hundred miles to deep waters east of the Bahamas, in the next two weeks. The Bahamian Coast Guard spotted them off the southern coast of Andros Island.

Meanwhile, back at MMC, an elderly female rough-tooth, affectionately known as Grandma, succumbed to multiple medical problems. A necropsy revealed that Grandma had eaten a number of beer cans in her lifetime—the most amazing, a pull-tab can that dated back many decades. (To a starving dolphin, the flash of sparkling aluminum may be indistinguishable from silvery fish scales.)

The remaining dolphins were nicknamed the "Fab Four Females" by their keepers. The young calf continued to thrive, eating three to four pounds of fish and five liters of formula a day. The other three ate six hearty meals daily—herring, sardines, smelt, and capelin—and appeared healthy and well adjusted in their temporary surroundings. On July 19, however, after 138 days of successful rehabilitation, R303 mysteriously died without showing any symptoms of distress. Her "family" at MMC was greatly saddened.

The young calf, never really knowing life in the ocean, could not be released in the wild. She joined another member of her species at a Florida captive facility in August. And in mid-September, after more than six months of rehabilitation, the final two female dolphins—Bumper and Belle—followed the release procedure of their predecessors and made their own trek back to the sea.

In all, eleven of the sixty-eight stranded rough-toothed dolphins returned to their home in the depths of the Atlantic. One lived on in captivity. Necropsy results finally showed that the fifty-seven deceased dolphins died from a number of different causes. Experts concluded, however, that the underlying reason for the stranding was probably starvation. For reasons still undetermined, the pod was not eating. The mystery continues.

RESOURCES

Hard Aground—1822

Borski, Jill Zima. "Alligator Nominated to Historic Places Register." *Tavernier Reporter,* October 3, 1996.

Dale, J.M., to military superiors in a letter. Norfolk, December 3, 1822.

Dean, Love. *Lighthouses of the Florida Keys.* Sarasota, FL: Pineapple Press, 1998.

Eyster, Irving R. "Alligator Light." *Tavernier Reporter,* July 13, 1996.

Mathewson, R. Duncan III. "The USS Alligator." *Islamorada Free Press,* August 1, 1990.

McCarthy, Kevin. *Thirty Florida Shipwrecks.* Sarasota, FL: Pineapple Press, 1992.

U.S. Naval Court of Inquiry, aboard U.S. Frigate *Guerrier,* December 10, 1822, transcript.

USS *Alligator* log. Norfolk, August 2 to November 9, 1822.

Viele, John, and Pam Viele. Compilation of contemporary newspaper accounts of loss of USS *Alligator* on Carysfort Reef, November 1822. Transcribed by Jim Clupper, Monroe County Public Library, Islamorada, Florida.

Doublecross—1827

Brothers, Betty. *Wreckers and Workers of Old Key West*. Big Pine Key, FL: privately printed, 1972.

Swanson, Gail. *Slave Ship Guerrero*. West Conshohocken, PA: Infinity Publishing Company, 2005.

Viele, John. *The Florida Keys*. Vol. 3. Sarasota, FL: Pineapple Press, 2001.

Massacre on Indian Key—1840

Carter, Kaye Edwards. *Rumskudgeon*. Hialeah, FL: B.P.K. Press, 1976.

Eyster, Irving R., and Darlene Brown. *Indian Key Massacre*. Annapolis, MD: U.S. Naval Institute Press: 1976.

Florida Department of Natural Resources. *History of Indian Key*, Florida Department of Natural Resources, Division of Recreation and Parks, Tallahassee.

Hardiman, Colleen. "The Terror of the Massacre on Indian Key." *Sundial*, July 31, 1983.

Lafferty, Michael. "Past Wreckers a Mixed Bag." *Sundial*, July 31, 1983.

Sundial. "A Grim Isle—Indian Key Early History." July 31, 1983.

Wilkinson, Jerry. "Charles Howe Jr. Letter of the Massacre," November 2, 1843, Florida Keys History Reading Room reprint of original manuscript, www.keyshistory.org/IK-Chas-Howe-Jr-Ltr.html.

———. "The Massacre Story." Florida Keys History Reading Room. www.keyshistory.org /IK-massacre-1.html. Reprint from *The Hollywood Magazine,* March 1, 1945, by Sarah W. Palmer.

———. "Sarah Walker Palmer's version of the Massacre at Indian Key." Florida Keys History Reading Room. www.keyshistory .org/IK-Sarah-massacre-1925.html.

The Key West Hooker Chronicles—1848

Adams, Earl R. "Gathering Sponges in the Keys Was Once a $450,000 Industry." *Key West Citizen,* November 30, 1978.

Brown, Neil. "The Greeks Are Coming, Spongers Say." *Miami Herald,* October 18, 1981.

Bureau of Seafood and Aquaculture Marketing, Florida Department of Agriculture and Consumer Services. www.fl-seafood.com/key_west.htm.

Burkett, Elinor. "Spongers at Work." *Miami Herald,* June 10, 1988.

Cappick, Mary Louise. "The Key West Story." Parts 45, 46. *Key West Coral Tribune,* July 1956, August 1958.

Dean, Love. "Sheepswool Sponges Resurface on Florida Keys." *Oceans Magazine,* March 1982.

———. "Sponger Money: It May Come Back." *Florida Keys Magazine,* 2nd Quarter, 1981.

Delp, Ron. "The Old Ways Still Works for Spongers." *Florida Keys Keynoter,* August 2, 1984.

Eyster, Irving R. "Sponging in the Keys." *Tavernier Reporter,* October 10, 1996.

Langley, Wright. "Sponging Adds to Income." *Miami Herald,* March 12, 1968.

Oleson, Russ. "Fishermen in the Florida Keys See Sponge Fishing Revive." *National Fisherman,* March 1982.

Osborne, Ozzie. "Sponging Absorbs Business As Old Rivals Sink." *Miami Herald,* November 19, 1989.

Scribner's Magazine. "Sponge and Spongers of the Florida Reef." November 1892.

Shubow, David. "Sponge Fishing on Florida's East Coast." *Tequesta—The Journal of the Historical Association of Southern Florida,* no. 29, Miami, 1969.

Viele, John. "Memories of Old Sugarloaf Key." *Florida Keys Keynoter,* February 5, 1997.

Williams, Betty. "The Sponging Trade Has Died But the Demand Still Thrives." *Key West Citizen,* September 23, 1977.

Witzell, W.N. "The Origin of the Florida Sponge Fishery." *Marine Fisheries Review* 60, no. 1 (1998): 27–32.

Muddied Waters—1865

"The Famous Prisoner of Fort Jefferson." www.fastcatferry.com/mudd.htm.

Steers, Edward Jr. *His Name Is Still Mudd.* Gettysburg, PA: Thomas Publications, 1997.

Summers, Robert K. *Dr. Samuel A. Mudd at Fort Jefferson.* North Charleston, SC: Book-Surge, 2005.

Up in Smoke—1886
Adams, Earl R. "Cigar Making Once Was Island's Biggest Industry." *Key West Citizen,* January 27, 1977.

Boese, Ann. "A Key to History." *Cigar Aficionado,* November/December 1997.

Brothers, Betty. *Wreckers and Workers of Old Key West.* Big Pine Key, FL: printed privately, 1972.

Brown, Jefferson B. *Key West—The Old and the New.* Gainesville: University of Florida Press, 1973.

Canon, Warren. "Tobacco Leaves Key West." *Key West Citizen,* January 1, 1976.

Caputo, Marc. "Cigar Roller Recalls Industry's Heyday of Wealth, Prominence." *Key West Citizen,* October 15, 1991.

Eldredge, Bill. "Cigars Were Big Business." *Florida Keys Keynoter,* November 22, 1979.

Hogan, Michael. "Cigars: Another Key West/Cuba Connection." *Key West Island Life,* January 23, 1992.

Provenzo, Eugene F. Jr., and Concepción N. Garcia. "Cigar Rolling . . . a Craft Fading into History." *Tabascos Maribel Miami Update* 7, no. 3 (August 1980).

Smith, Anne. "He Read Romance into Tough Life of Cigar Workers." *Miami Herald,* June 3, 1966.

Swanson, Brad. "Cigar-Maker's Hands Remember." *Miami Herald,* June 24, 1979.

Thompson, Martha, and David Johnson. "Once the King of Key West, the Craft of Cigar Making Is a Dead Art Now." *Florida Keys Magazine,* 3rd Quarter, 1980.

Westfall, Loy Glenn. *Key West, Cigar City USA.* Book 1 of trilogy, self-published, 1997.

Bradley's Bird Battle—1905

Benz, Stephen. "The Feather Wars." *Tropic, Miami Herald* Sunday Magazine, September 22, 1996.

Daily Miami Metropolis. "Guy Bradley Was Wounded." July 14, 1905.

———. "Guy Bradley Was Killed Instantly." July 15, 1905.

———. "Guy Bradley and the Plume Hunters." Florida Audubon Society, July 3–September 1, 1986.

Harold, Rosemary. "Naturalist's Life and Death Shown for Audubon 100th." *Miami Herald,* July 9, 1986.

Keating, Dan. "County Honors Dead Officers." *Miami Herald,*
    May 14, 1993.

McIver, Stuart, "Death of a Bird Warden." *South Florida History,*
    Fall 2001.

————. "Plume Hunt on Cypress Creek." *Miami Magazine.*

Schwiep, Paul J. "Milady's Plumes and Boas Cost Bird Protector
    His Life." *Miami Herald,* July 8, 1995.

Wilbanks, Dr. Wm. "Guy M. Bradley." *Florida Keys Sea Heritage
    Journal* 6, no.1 (1995): 9–14.

First Train to Paradise—1912
Chandler, David Leon. *Henry Flagler, The Astonishing Life and
    Times of the Visionary Robber Baron Who Founded Florida.* New
    York: Macmillan Publishing Co., 1986.

Hopkins, Alice. "The Development of The Overseas Highway."
    Tequesta—The Journal of the Historical Association of Southern
    Florida, vol. 46, 1986, Miami.

Parks, Pat. *The Railroad That Died at Sea.* Brattleboro, VT: Steven
    Greene Press, 1968.

Standiford, Les. *Last Train to Paradise.* New York: Three Rivers
    Press, 2002.

Thompson, Marvin. "The First and Last Trains." *Key West Citizen,*
    March 6, 1967.

Wilkinson, Jerry. "History of the Railroad." Florida Keys History Reading Room, www.keyshistory.org/flagler.html.

Wilkinson, "K". *It Had to Be You.* Bellingham, WA: Sunshine Printing, 1996.

Mosquitoes 1, Bats 0—1929

Harrigan, Peter. "Efforts Are Underway to Restore Sugarloaf's Famous Bat Tower." *Miami Herald,* February 20, 1980.

Kiser, Mark. "Dr. Charles Campbell: Bat House Pioneer." *Bat Conservation International, Inc.,* 2002.

Klingener, Nancy. "Batty Idea to Fight Mosquitoes Catches On." *Miami Herald,* March 9, 1997.

Lane, Christopher. "Bees Get Boot at Bat Tower." *Miami Herald,* June 9, 1981.

Mohr, Charles E. *The World of the Bat.* Philadelphia: J.B. Lippincott Company, 1976.

Viele, John. "1930s Sugarloaf Life Isolated But Civilized." *Island Navigator,* May 1991.

Wadlow, Kevin. "Bat Tower History Recalled by Builder." *Florida Keys Keynoter,* February 25, 1982.

Williams, Joy. *The Florida Keys.* New York: Random House, 1996.

Blind Pigs and Bootleg—1933

Banks, Ann. *First-Person America.* New York: Random House, 1981.

Beare, Nikki. *Pirates, Pineapples, and People.* Miami Beach: Atlantic Publishing Company, 1961.

Carter, James A. "Florida and Rum Running." *Florida Historical Quarterly,* July 1969.

Garnett, Burt. "Rum-running in the Economy of the Keys." Key West Havana Cigar Company. "Raul Vasquez" page. www .keywestfolkart.com/vasquez.htm. Article reprinted from Martello, vol. 4 (1967).

Gibbs, Steve. "Smuggling in the Keys." *Islamorada Free Press,* February 4, 1998.

"History of Sloppy Joe's." Sloppy Joe's. www.sloppyjoes.com/ history.htm.

"If the Walls Could Talk," Captain Tony's Saloon. www.capttonys saloon.com.

Jacobsen, Frank. "Retired 'Revenooer' Recalls Key West in Prohibition Days." *Key West Citizen,* May 22, 1960.

"Rum War: The U.S. Coast Guard & Prohibition." Donald L. Canney. www.uscg.mil/history/h_rumwar.html.

Smith, Anne. "'Deacon' Recalls Keys Rum Runs." *Miami Herald,* October 22, 1966.

Willoughby, Malcolm F. *Rum War at Sea*. U.S. Treasury Department, Washington DC: U.S. Government Printing Office, 1964.

Mother Nature's Fury—1935

"1935 Labor Day Hurricane," www.overseasrailroad.railfan.net/1935hurr.htm.

"1935 Storm Swept Away All But Memories." *USA Today*. www.usatoday.printthis.clickability.com.

Eyster, Irving. "Junction City, Great Depression, Labor Day Hurricane and Tolls." *Islamorada Free Press*, November 17, 1999.

Klingener, Nancy. "'It Felt Like Eternity. Like Forever': Keys to the Past, An Oral History." *Miami Herald*, July 2, 1995.

Klinkenberg, Jeff. "Killer in the Keys." *St. Petersburg Times*, August 14, 1991.

"Labor Day Hurricane of 1935." www.wikipedia.com.

McDonald, W.F. "The Hurricane of August 31 to September 6, 1935." *Hurricane Monthly Review*, 1935.

Mencke, Scott. "Man of the Sea." *Florida Keys Keynoter*, October 27, 1990.

Pervis, Jones A., and James O. Duncan. Alligator Reef Lighthouse Keeper's Log, Sept. 1–2, 1935, transcript in Monroe County Public Library, Islamorada, FL.

Platero, John. "After 50 Years, Recalling a Day of Death on the Keys." *Washington Post,* September 1, 1985.

Standiford, Les. *Last Train to Paradise.* New York: Three Rivers Press, 2002.

Watson, Stephanie. "1935 Labor Day Hurricane." www.weather .com/newscenter/specialreports/sotc/storm1/page1.html.

Against All Protocol—1943

Atwood, Anthony YNC. "An Incident at Sea: The Historic Combat between U.S. Navy Blimp K-74 and U-Boat 134." Master's thesis, Florida International University, 2003.

———. "The Battle between the Blimp and Sub." *Aviation News,* March/April 1997.

Sotham, John. "From This Naval Air Station Airships Hunted U-Boats in the Florida Keys." *Air and Space Magazine,* August/September 2001.

Thompson, Dick. "SOS over Sonar Signals." *Boat/US Magazine,* July 2005.

Vaeth, J. Gordon. "Incident in the Florida Straits." *Proceedings,* August 1979.

Island at War—1962

"Army Leases Wickers Field for $1 a Year." *Key West Citizen,* October 25, 1962.

Brugioni, Dino A. "The Invasion of Cuba." *MHQ—The Quarterly Journal of Military History* 4, no. 2 (1992).

Diamond, Aviva. "When Key West Was on Front Lines." *Miami Herald,* October 24, 1976.

Greene, Juanita. "Everybody Was Shook Up Until the Big Chief Arrived." *Miami Herald,* November 30, 1962.

"Jets Were Kept Busy." *Key West Citizen,* November 27, 1962.

Kennedy, John Fitzgerald. "The U.S. Response to Soviet Military Buildup in Cuba—President Kennedy's Report to the People." Washington, DC: U.S. Department of State, October 22, 1962.

Kersey, Kay. "Aid Given to Carry Message to Cubans." *Key West Citizen,* October 23, 1962.

Key Outpost. "Naval Base Welcomes President Kennedy." November 30, 1962.

Key West Citizen. "Casa Marina Turned over to Military," October 25, 1962.

———. "Kennedy Sees Hope for Crisis Solution," October 28, 1962.

———. "Key West Watches Calmly," October 28, 1962.

Koslow, Bob. "Missiles Brought Military." *Florida Keys Keynoter,* November 25, 1987.

Noriega, Saturnino. "Week Makes Many Changes." *Key West Citizen,* October 28, 1962.

Quickstad, Sheila. "Key West: Nearest to War 16 Years Ago Today."
Key West Citizen, October 22, 1978.

Pinder, Don. "For Fidel, with Love . . ." *Key West Citizen,* November 1, 1962.

"Planes Pour into Key West." *Miami Herald,* October 24, 1962.

Sosin, Milt. "Key West Ball Park Gone." *Key West Citizen,* October 23, 1962.

Trumbell, Stephen. "Natty Boca Chica Pipes Its Chief Aboard."
Miami Herald, November 27, 1962.

Wilkinson, Jerry. "History of the North Key Largo Missile Site."
Florida Keys History Reading Room. www.keyshistory.org/KL-NikeSite.html.

Flotilla to Freedom—1980

Amlong, William R., and Guillermo Martínez. "First Victims of
Cuban Exodus: 2 Bodies in Boat off Key West." *Miami Herald,*
April 29, 1980.

Fiedler, Tom. "Emergency Declared in Florida." *Miami Herald,*
January 1981.

Chapman, Tim. "I Saw Joy, Sadness, Weariness, and Hope." *Miami
Herald.* April 3, 2005. www.miami.com/mld/miamiherald/news
/special_packages/mariel/11288486.

Hume, David, and Robert Rivas. "First Refugees Reach Keys—By
Boat." *Miami Herald,* April 22, 1980.

Fix, Janet L. "To Get the Story, I Hid on a Boat Near Mariel." *Miami Herald,* April 3, 2005. www.miami.com/mld/miami herald/news/special_packages/mariel/11288485.

Key West Citizen. "Castro Says U.S. Took Cuba's Scum," December, 18, 1980.

Martenhoff, Jim. "The Freedom Fleet." *Yachting Magazine,* July 1980.

Miami Herald. "Carter Orders Flotilla's End," May 15, 1980.

Nielsen, John, with Jerry Buckley in Key West, John Taylor in New York, and Ojito Mirta Smith. *Finding Mañana.* New York: Penguin Press, 2005.

Powell, Jerry. "Boat Seizures Protested." *Florida Keys Keynoter,* July 3, 1980.

Rivas, Robert. "Four Cubans Hijack Boat to Freedom." *Miami Herald,* July 10, 1980.

Rivas, Robert, and Ivan A. Castro. "Key West Again a Refugee Hub." *Miami Herald,* April 24, 1980.

Stabile, VADM Benedict L., USCG (Ret.), and Dr. Robert L. Scheina. "U.S. Coast Guard Operations during the 1980 Cuban Exodus." U.S. Coast Guard. www.uscg.mil/hq/g-cp/history/USCG_Mariel_History_1980.html.

Tasker, Frederic, and Guillermo Martínez. "Boats Carry Hundreds of Cubans This Way." *Miami Herald,* April 23, 1980.

Vern, E. "Sea Lift from Cuba to Key West." *Newsweek,* May 5, 1980.

Whitefield, Mimi. "Mariel vs. Today's Exodus—Similar, Different." *Miami Herald,* August 26, 1994.

Windhorn, Stan. "More Boats in Havana Port Awaiting Refugee Transport." *Key West Citizen,* April 29, 1980.

If at First You Don't Secede . . . —1982

Anderson, Peter. "The Conch Republic." www.conchrepublic.com/the_beginning.htm.

Islamorada Free Press. "Conch Republic Celebrated," May 1, 1991.

Key Largo Independent. "The Conch Republic—Old Enough to Drink," April 23, 2003.

King, Gregory. *The Conch That Roared.* Lexington, KY: Weston and Wright, 1997.

Klingener, Nancy. "10-Year-Old Conch Republic Lives On." *Miami Herald,* April 15, 1992.

Linn's Stamp News. "USPS Gives Informal Recognition to Conch," January 30, 1983.

White, Brooks. "History of the Conch Republic—Key West and the Florida Keys." www.members.aol.com/brooks957/crhist.htm.

Finders Keepers—1985

Bolan, Mandy. "Island Mourns for Mel." *Key West Citizen,* December 1998.

Klingener, Nancy. "No More Holes in Sea Bottom, Fisher Warned." *Miami Herald,* July 28, 1992.

———. "Treasure Hunter Passes into Legend." *Miami Herald,* December 21, 1998.

Lund, Ted. "New Trove of Atocha Located, Team Says." *Miami Herald,* July 2000.

Lynch, Marika. "Treasure Hunters Must Give Up Loot." *Miami Herald,* July 31, 1997.

McHaley, Bleth, and Wendy Tucker. *The Mel Fisher Story.* Key West, FL: Salvors Inc., 1991.

"Mel's Story—Today's the Day." Crystals, Inc. www.melfisher.com/salvage/go/melstory.asp.

Miami Herald. "Underwater Gold Rush," July 2000.

Ornstein, Susan. "Atocha's Treasure-filled Chests Recovered." *Miami Herald,* July 27, 1985.

———. "Captain Says He Did It for His Dad." *Miami Herald,* August 29, 1985.

———. "Corks Fly as Investors Finally Lay Claim to Booty." *Miami Herald,* October 17, 1986.

"The Search Begins—Story of Mel Fisher." Rare Atocha Coins. www.rareatochacoins.com.

Shillington, Patty. "Treasure Hunters Strike Gold Off Key West." *Miami Herald,* July 21, 1985.

Sullivan, George. *Treasure Hunt.* Port Salerno, FL: Florida Classics Library, 1987.

The Prez and Grey's Ghosts—1989

Adler, Dick. "Zane Grey and Long Key Fishing Club." Duck Key Online. www.duckkeyonline.com/duck_key_history/zane_grey.htm.

Benedetto, Richard. "Pool Report from Air Force Two." Typewritten transcript. January 13, 1989.

Dean, Love. "Grey, The Upper Keys' Most Famous Fisherman." *Islamorada Free Press,* January 22, 1999.

Eyster, Irving R. "Long Key History Pre-Dates Pilgrims." *Tavernier Reporter,* January 4, 1998.

Foley, Phil. "Bush Bags Two Tarpon during Fishing Trip." *Florida Keys Keynoter,* April 27, 1988.

———. "Bush Gives Thumbs Up on Keys Visit." *Florida Keys Keynoter,* January 18, 1989.

———. "Keys Get Ready for Bush Visit." *Florida Keys Keynoter,* January 14, 1989.

———. "Keys Prepare for Bush Visit." *Florida Keys Keynoter,* January 11, 1989.

———. "President-elect Bush Reels in the Fish." *Florida Keys Keynoter,* January 18, 1989.

———. "President-elect Is Headed Here." *Florida Keys Keynoter,* January 7, 1989.

———. "Press Enjoys Respite from the Cold North." *Florida Keys Keynoter,* January 18, 1989.

———. "Will Keys Be 'Little White House'?" *Florida Keys Keynoter,* November 11, 1988.

Grey, Zane. "The Barracuda of Long Key." *Field and Stream,* July 1912.

———. "Tales of Fishes." *Outdoorsman.* New York: Grosset & Dunlap, 1919.

Long Key Fishing Club. *Long Key Fishing Club Manual,* 1934–35.

McLendon, James. *Pioneer in the Florida Keys—The Life and Times of Del Layton.* Miami: E.A. Seeman, 1976.

Sand, George. "A Fishing President—It's about Time!" *Muskie,* 1989.

Schaeffer, Dorothy. "Long Key Fishing Club." *Humm's Guide,* Fall 1989.

Wilkinson, Jerry. "History of Long Key." Florida Keys History Reading Room. www.keyshistory.org /longkey.html.

Drowning the *African Queen*—1992

"The African Queen." www.wikipedia.com.

Associated Press, " 'African Queen' Steaming Again in Key Largo." *St. Petersburg Times,* January 8, 1984.

Delaney, Dr. Dudley. "The African Queen." *Engineers & Engines,* July–August 1974.

Foley, Phil. "The 'Queen' Sinks." *Florida Keys Keynoter,* May 20, 1992.

Klinkenberg, Marty, "The 'African Queen' Stays Afloat – in Key Largo." *Honolulu Star-Bulletin,* Cox News Service, June 1, 1984.

A Tale of True Lies—1993

Capuzzo, Mike. "Building the Seven Mile Bridge." *Tropic,* April 18, 1982.

Detwiler, Eric. "Keys to Experience Sights, Sounds of Movie Making at Close Range." *Key West Citizen,* November 18, 1993.

———. "Terrorists Converge." *Key West Citizen,* November 19, 1993.

Florida Keys Keynoter. "Are You Ready for Arnold in the Keys?" July 8, 1994.

Hollander, Sarah. " 'Terrorism School.'" *Key West Citizen,* November 1993.

Kubicek, Margaret. "Two Thumbs Up!" *Key West Citizen,* July 10, 1994.

Larson, Luisa. "Bombs Away for Arnold and Co." *Florida Keys Keynoter,* October 27, 1993.

"Seven Mile Bridge." www.wikipedia.com.

Steinman, Jon. "'True Lies' Sets July Release Date." *Key West Citizen,* May 22, 1994.

True Lies. Lighthouse Productions, Twentieth Century Fox, 1994.

Wadlow, Kevin. "Built on a Whim, Bridge Lives On." *Florida Keys Keynoter,* May 20, 1982.

———. "Movie 'Attack' Noise Worries Sugarloaf." *Florida Keys Keynoter,* November 29, 1993.

West, Jon. "Options Available for Moser Boaters." *Florida Keys Keynoter,* November 17, 1993.

On Her Side—2002

"A Fascinating Dive Opportunity Takes a Turn for the Better." Monroe County Tourist Development Council. Spiegel Grove Wreck pages. www.fla-keys.com/spiegelgrove/spiegel_funds.cfm.

"Cleaning 510-foot-long Spiegel Grove Required Work of Industrial Demolition Company." Monroe County Tourist Development Council. Speigel Grove Wreck pages. www.fla-keys .com/spiegelgrove /spiegel_cleaning.cfm.

"Divers and Snorkelers Flock to the Spiegel Grove Wreck." Monroe County Tourist Development Council. Speigel Grove Wreck pages. www.fla-keys.com/spiegelgrove/spiegel_retired.cfm.

"Diving on the Spiegel Grove." Monroe County Tourist Development Council. Speigel Grove Wreck pages. www.fla-keys.com/spiegelgrove/spiegel_diving.cfm.

"The Eight-Year Effort to Sink the Spiegel Grove." Monroe County Tourist Development Council. Speigel Grove Wreck pages. www.fla-keys.com/spiegelgrove.

"Keys Community Came Together to Fund Artificial Reef Project." Monroe County Tourist Development Council. Speigel Grove Wreck pages. www.fla-keys.com/spiegelgrove/spiegel_cleaning.cfm.

"Spiegel Grove Fast Facts." Monroe County Tourist Development Council. Speigel Grove Wreck pages. www.fla-keys.com/spiegelgrove /spiegel_fastfacts.cfm.

"Spiegel Grove Fulfilling Mission as Dive Attraction and Fish Magnet." Monroe County Tourist Development Council. Speigel Grove Wreck pages. www.fla-keys.com/spiegelgrove.

"Spiegel Grove History . . . Sinking of Cold War Relic Stirs Memories," Monroe County Tourist Development Council. Speigel Grove Wreck pages. www.fla-keys.com/spiegelgrove.

"Spiegel Grove Now Upright Courtesy of Dennis, Re-opens to Divers." Monroe County Tourist Development Council. Speigel Grove Wreck pages. www.fla-keys.com/spiegelgrove.

Ruffled Feathers—2004

"BBC News," transcript, April 20, 2006.

Buckley, Cara. "Chicken Magnet: Key West Barber Gains Fame with Job Trapping Wily." *Milwaukee Journal Sentinel,* February 22, 2004.

"CBS News," transcript, April 13, 2006.

The Chicken Store. www.thechickenstore.com.

"City of Key West Code of Ordinances, Title V, Public Health. 5300 Animal Control. Part II. Key West Chickens. www.keywest chickens.com /city.php.

"Countdown with Keith Olbermann," MSNBC, transcript, March 25, 2004.

"CNN Sunday Morning," transcript, February 15, 2004.

Crossen, Cynthia. "Key West Chickens May Run Afoul of Bird-Flu Fears." *Pittsburgh Post-Gazette,* March 16, 2006.

Degler, Ward. "Free-roaming Key West Chickens Cause a Squawk— Again." *Zionsville Time Sentinel.* www.timessentinel.com.

Gallagher, Tara L. "Operation Chicken Snatch." *Animal Welfare Institute Quarterly* 51, no. 2 (Spring 2002).

"The Key West 'Chicken Wars.'" www.jewelrygenius.com/ aaNEWHTMLS/ROOSTER/chicken wars.html.

Key West Citizen. Editorial. "Southernmost Poultry Have Our Full Attention." January 10, 2004.

Lush, Tamara. "Key West Wants Chickens Shipped Away." *St. Petersburg Times,* January 13, 2004.

Mott, Maryann. "Bird Flu Fears May Clip the Wings of Key West Chickens." *National Geographic News,* April 28, 2006.

O'Hara, Timothy. "Chicken Catching Idea Wins Approval." *Key West Citizen,* January 7, 2004. www.livableoldtown .com//chicken_catching_idea.htm.

————. "City Hires Chicken Catcher." *Key West Citizen,* January 21, 1004. www.livableoldtown.com/city_hires_chicken_ catcher.htm.

————. "City Officials, Parra Disagree on How to Fend Off Fowl." *Key West Citizen,* July 23, 2004.

————. "Eviction Looms for City's Chickens." *Key West Citizen,* January 4, 1004. www.livableoldtown.com/eviction_looms.htm.

O'Neal, Rob. "For the Birds." *Key West Citizen,* January 14, 2004.

Pacenti, John. "Chickens Have Key West Squawking." *Detroit News.* Associated Press, www.shanmonster.com.

Tedesco, Carol. "Snowbird Column Reflects 'Them vs. Us' Attitude." *Key West Citizen,* January 24, 2004.

Marooned in Marathon—2005
"All Things Considered," transcript, National Public Radio, March 21, 2005.

"Dolphins' Beaching Closely Followed Sub's Exercises."
www.nbc6.net, March 6, 2005.

"Four Dolphins Remain in Rehab after Mass Stranding."
www.nbc6.net, June 17, 2005.

Hobbs, Barbara. "Notch and Naia: A Remembrance in Three
Parts." Petersburg Marine Mammal Center, www.psgmmc.org.

"Marine Mammal Stranding." www.dolphins.org.

"Navy Investigates Sonar Role in Dolphin Strandings."
www.nbc6.net, March 9, 2005.

"Organization Needs Supplies, Volunteers in Effort to Save Dolphins." www.nbc6.net, March 11, 2005.

"Rescue and Rehab." Marine Mammal Conservancy, 2006.
www.marinemammalconscrvancy.org.

"Rescuers Continue Effort to Save Beached Dolphins."
www.nbc6.net, March 2, 2005.

"Rough-Tooth Dolphin Gives Birth to Stillborn Calf."
www.nbc6.net, March 7, 2005.

"Rough Toothed Dolphin Mass Stranding Event—March 2, 2005,"
transcript, Public Debriefing, August 24, 2005.

"Seven Rehabilitated Dolphins Released." www.nbc6.net, May 3,
2005.

"Seven Rehabilitated Dolphins Tracked Near Bahamas, Cuba."
www.nbc6.net, May 11, 2005.

"Several Dolphins Unexpectedly Give Birth after Being Stranded." www.nbc6.net, March 8, 2005.

Sherriff, Lucy. "U.S. Navy Sued over Dolphin-Stranding Sonar." *The Register,* www.theregister.co.uk, October 20, 2005.

Thompson, Dick. "SOS over Sonar Signals." *Boat/US Magazine,* July 2005.

"Two Dolphins Released after Mass Stranding." www.nbc6.net, April 20, 2005.

"Volunteers Needed in Continuing Dolphin Rescue Effort." www.nbc6.net, March 7, 2005.

"Weather Hampers Dolphin Rescue Efforts." www.nbc6.net, March 4, 2005.

Zarrella, John. "Stranded Dolphins Get Round-the-Clock Care." www.cnn.com, April 14, 2005.

INDEX

ABOUT THE AUTHOR

A University of Wisconsin graduate, Victoria Shearer was a teacher briefly and then became an advertising account executive in Fairfield County, Connecticut, outside New York City. In the late 1980s, she was copy editor for *COOK'S* magazine. In the early 1990s she lived in London, combining her passion for food with that of travel as she launched her on-going career as a freelance writer, producing feature articles for newspapers and magazines across the United States. Victoria is the author of twelve editions of the *Insiders' Guide to the Florida Keys and Key West* and *The Florida Keys Cookbook—Recipes and Foodways of Paradise,* as well as *Walking Places in New England.*

Fascinated by the diverse history of the Florida Keys, Victoria immersed herself in the archives of the Key Largo, Islamorada, Marathon, and Key West libraries for two years, writing *It Happened in the Florida Keys.* Hidden within the yellowed newspaper clippings, she discovered tales of triumph and tragedy, inspiration and indignation, courage and comedy—threads of happenstance woven through the years into the unique fabric that makes up the Florida Keys.

Victoria and her husband, Bob, have enjoyed the beauty and bounty of the Keys for more than twenty years. They have two children and six grandchildren.